LEGENDARY WHITETAILS

LEGENDARY WHITETAILS

Mequon, Wisconsin

LEGENDARY WHITETAILS
Stories And Photos Of 40 Of The Greatest Bucks Of All Time
Copyright © 1996 by Wildlife Images

Compiled by: Larry L. Huffman
Edited by: Gordon Whittington & David Morris

Contributing Writers:
Les Davenport, Duncan Dobie, Jack Ehresman, Brad Herndon, Dick Idol,
Greg Miller, Jeff Murray, Dr. Rob Wegner, and Bill Winke.

Published by Larry L. Huffman of Wildlife Images,
1115 West Liebau Road in Mequon, WI 53092,
in cooperation with Venture Press and
North American WHITETAIL magazine.

Printed in the United States of America
Fourth Edition
Printed in 2008

Library of Congress Catalog Card Number: 95-62041
ISBN 0-9633315-3-1

Dedication

This book is dedicated to all the hunters featured between these covers. Their accomplishment in the field has brought much wonder, joy and sense of anticipation to all who take to the woods each fall with a gun or bow.

Finally and most importantly, this book is dedicated to our Lord Jesus Christ, who made it all possible by creating the magnificent whitetail deer.

ACKNOWLEDGEMENTS

BY LARRY HUFFMAN

It has been my privilege to work with some of the finest people in the business in making this book a reality. Without their contribution, this book would not have been possible. The number of people involved is legion, and I can't possibly name them all. But here, I do want to extend a special thanks to the main players:

First and foremost, to my partner in this venture and good friend, Dick Idol. Dick's undying interest in giant whitetails was a principal factor in uncovering many of the trophy bucks featured here. No one knows these deer better than Dick Idol. His contribution was immeasurable.

To David Morris, also my partner in this book and the publisher. David's knowledge of the whitetail and expertise in publishing made putting this book together both enjoyable and relatively painless.

To Steve Vaughn and his staff at Game & Fish Publications. They provided assistance and the utmost cooperation in the reprinting of several feature articles from past issues of *North American WHITETAIL* magazine.

To Gordon Whittington, editor of *North American WHITETAIL* magazine. His professionalism in editing this book showed why he is considered the best in the business.

To the contributing authors, Greg Miller, Dr. Rob Wegner, Les Davenport, Duncan Dobie, Brad Herndon, Bill Winke, Jeff Murray and Jack Ehresman. Their research, knowledge and writing expertise are much appreciated.

To the great taxidermists, Joe Meder, Tom Sexten, Gary Bowen, Locie Murphy, Gary Koc and Jack Lemke, who worked on the "Legendary Collection."

To Gary Donald, who willingly shared his tremendous knowledge of Canadian bucks, and to Dr. Chuck Arnold for providing information about certain bucks in the collection.

To Jack Reneau and his staff at the Boone and Crockett Club for providing scores, and to friends Bill Lilienthal and Dave Boland for scoring help and encouragement.

To the many hunters featured in this book who allowed us to share in their great adventure and accomplishment.

To my sons, Greg and Troy Huffman. They eagerly provided help and encouragement all the way through.

To Tom Johnson, the manager of Wildlife Images. He invested countless hours into this publication.

To friend and hunting companion Bob Smith for his help displaying the collection at whitetail exhibits, and to the members of the Wisconsin Buck and Bear Club for their assistance.

To Ron Brown, the photographer who, unless otherwise indicated, captured all of the great images that lead off the chapters.

Finally, to Joyce, my wife and companion of over 40 years, for putting up with my love for whitetails. She has patiently endured my many hours devoted to various trophy whitetail projects, though I must admit she has questioned my sanity from time to time.

TABLE OF CONTENTS

The word "legend" is defined as "a story of some wonderful event handed down for generations among people and popularly believed to have a historical basis."

from the Foreword by Larry Huffman

PREFACE

By David Morris

When Dick Idol, Larry Huffman and I first discussed the idea of putting together a book featuring the "Legendary Whitetail Collection," three thoughts came to mind immediately. One, this was a chance to capture whitetail hunting history and lore in a way never done before. Two, the book would become a treasured classic that would be passed on from generation to generation. Three, I definitely wanted to be a part of it.

With the decision made to go forward, I immediately called Steve Vaughn, my partner at *North American WHITE-TAIL,* and he eagerly joined forces with us on the project. After all, *WHITETAIL* was the publication that first introduced many of the bucks in the Legendary Whitetail Collection to an avid deer hunting market. Since nobody knew these bucks better than *WHITETAIL* editor Gordon Whittington, we sought his editorial expertise, which he gladly offered. Soon, we were underway.

Talk about a team! Larry Huffman, who owns the Legendary Whitetail Collection, which counts among its numbers some of the most impressive and famous whitetails of all time. Dick Idol, one of the first and most knowledgeable giant buck enthusiasts who originally discovered and previously owned many of the deer in the collection. Gordon Whittington, who is nothing short of a walking encyclopedia when it comes to world-class deer. Throw in Tom Bulloch, a topnotch designer, as well as an ace deer hunter, who knew exactly how to showcase these great bucks on the printed page. Add to these guys the combined resources of *North American WHITETAIL* and Venture Press, and the book born of the joint efforts has to be something special. And, it is!

The greatest bucks of all time are here—the Jordan, the Breen, the Hole-In-The-Horn, the Austin, the Bills, the Raveling, the Kohler, the list goes on, including the current world record typical and non-typical. This book is about the legendary bucks, not just big bucks, but the ones that die-hard trophy hunters across the continent know by sight and name. They are a part of our hunting tradition and belong to all who pull on those long-handles in the predawn darkness and strike out into the cold woods, hoping…

So, if you've ever dreamed of having a monster whitetail buck walk out in front of you…if you've ever marveled at the uniqueness and beauty of a giant whitetail rack…if you've ever harbored the hope that maybe, just maybe someday you'll find yourself kneeling beside a buck that is simply too big to believe, **Legendary Whitetails** is for you. This is a book of dreams come true.

"The greatest bucks of all time are here—the Jordan, the Breen, the Hole-In-The-Horn, the Austin, the Bills, the Raveling, the Kohler, the list goes on, including the current world record typical and non-typical."

FOREWORD

BY LARRY L. HUFFMAN

"Legendary whitetails." Exactly what are legendary whitetails? Webster's Dictionary describes the word "legendary" as "based on or presented in a legend or legends." The word "legend" is defined as "a story of some wonderful event handed down for generations among people and popularly believed to have a historical basis."

As I began assembling the Legendary Whitetail Collection featured in this book, one of my prime considerations was that each buck must have a unique history and story that would indeed qualify it as a "legendary whitetail." I believe this goal has been met.

The Jim Jordan Buck, with its almost bizarre story, certainly exemplifies this. Soon after being shot in 1914, the buck was taken to a taxidermist, who promptly disappeared with the buck. It remained unknown to the world for 50 years before resurfacing in 1964 to become the world record typical. Upon its reappearing, Jim Jordan, 50 years after shooting the buck, recognized his long-lost deer. Sadly, he spent his last remaining years trying to convince the

world he was indeed the hunter who had shot the largest typical of all time. Such is the stuff of legend.

Many of these legendary bucks were harvested by experienced, knowledgeable hunters. Several were hunted relentlessly for two, three or even four or more years. Curt Van Lith was one of those hunters who pursued a particular buck for several years before finally getting him. His great typical buck is tied for second place in the Pope and Young records.

It was not always the one who had pursued the buck for years, however, that ultimately claimed him. This was the case with the buck known as "Old Mossy Horns," which holds the top spot for archery non-typicals. The buck had been hunted by several hunters, but one in particular, Al Dawson, pursued him relentlessly for five years before his friend, Del Austin, arrowed the nine-year-old buck in 1962.

Some bucks, as you would expect, were harvested by novice hunters, proving once again that luck plays an important role in taking a world-class trophy. For instance, in 1974, Wayne Bills was asked by some friends to go on a deer hunt. He was new to the sport and had never shot a deer. Wayne proceeded to kill the new Iowa state record typical!

The buck known as "Big Red" was a legend in Todd County, Kentucky, before he was ever even hunted. Kentucky had not had a hunting season for 40 years. Everyone knew about Big Red. When season finally was opened in 1964, hundreds of hunters were after this wide Kentucky legend. C. W. Shelton was the hunter in the right place at the right time.

The story of John Bush's buck is extremely interesting. The whitetail was shot way back in 1870 at Elk River, Minnesota. Bush traveled there to hunt deer by horse and wagon from his home in Ohio. Indeed, John Bush, who was a celebrated sportsman in his time, was obviously a very dedicated deer hunter.

Homer Pearson's great non-typical became a legend in Wisconsin shortly after he shot the buck back on November 28, 1937. A life-sized mount stood in the Buckhorn Bar in the town of Rice Lake for years. This buck is the only legendary buck I know of that was taken by a husband and wife hunting team. She drove the thickets for her husband and pushed the buck out to him. How is that for love?

One of the most bizarre bucks ever taken by a hunter was Sammy Walker's Louisiana freak. The buck is listed as unscorable; however, one scorer came up with a total of 291 3/8 non-typical points. This buck is the most talked about when displayed at shows. Sammy's story is a classic tale of Southern hound hunting.

Some of the bucks featured in this book were not harvested by hunters. The incredibly impressive buck known as the "Illinois Roadkill" met his demise on the

bumper of a farmer's vehicle. The Lobster Claw Buck, so named because of his giant, forked drop tine, likely died of old age and was picked up by a young boy.

One of the most interesting bucks featured in these pages was actually a pen-raised deer by the name of "Desi." Desi died during his twelfth year; however, he sported his most impressive set of antlers during his tenth year. That giant rack scored 296 non-typical points. Amazingly, we have every set of antlers this buck grew and, with them, can actually follow the yearly development of a world-class buck.

Perhaps the most legendary of all is the Hole-In-The-Horn Buck from Ohio. This tremendous non-typical has 37 abnormal points totalling an unbelievable 192 7/8 inches, bringing his net non-typical score to a phenomenal 328 2/8. This magnificent buck was found dead near a railroad track in the early 1940s. In one of his massive drop tines was found a hole, from which the buck got his name. How that hole came to be has long been a mystery that has spawned much speculation. But just recently, that mystery has been solved...by an eyewitness no less! You'll find the answer later in this book. The great stories go on and on—more than 40 in total.

As I began putting the Legendary Whitetail Collection together, my dream was that someday it would be assembled in a public museum as an educational exhibit of interest to both the hunter and non-hunter. I'm still working to accomplish that, but in a way, this book, which does in fact put the deer on display for all to enjoy, is certainly a step toward fulfilling my dreams. Enjoy.

THE WORLD RECORD TYPICAL AND NON-TYPICAL

The Greatest Legends Of Them All

BY GORDON WHITTINGTON

Every sport has its legends, a handful of individuals who in their day towered above the crowd. Babe Ruth, Joe Montana, Wilt Chamberlain, Jack Nicklaus—athletes so renowned that even the casual fan can recall many of their achievements. It's as though these giants are sent along every so often to refresh us on what excellence really is.

So it is in the world of the white-tailed deer, as well. Although countless fine bucks have been taken to taxidermy shops over the years, only a few dozen of these deer can objectively be called "legends." And make no mistake, the greatest bucks are indeed just that. In their own way, these animals are every bit as special to deer hunters as the Babe is to baseball fans.

What makes a buck a legend? Actually, the process is much the same as with

On November 23, 1993, Saskatchewan deer hunter Milo Hanson rewrote whitetail history when he shot this 213 5/8-point buck to establish a new typical world record. Photo courtesy Boone and Crockett Club.

superstar athletes. First, there must be that just-right mixture of genes—a happy accident of heredity, if you will. But that alone won't do it. Many athletes and whitetails alike have been born with the potential to be great, only to fall short. There also must be optimum conditions for development, so that the individual's full potential can be realized. And then must come still another critical step: At precisely the right moment, the deer, just like the athlete, has to be given a stage upon which to develop and display his remarkable gift.

Sadly, fate often fails to allow this last scenario. Like a talented pitcher who, for one reason or another, never gets to take the mound, many phenomenal bucks no doubt have faded from whitetail history without ever having actually entered it.

The possible pitfalls are many. Perhaps a buck has the right genes to someday become a high-ranking trophy but is harvested before being given enough time to demonstrate his full potential. Maybe he actually reaches prime age but, because of the luck of the draw, lives out his life in an area with too little of the right food for maximum antler growth. Or, it could be that he actually grows an enormous rack, only to die of natural causes and never found by a human. And then, there's one other possibility—a situation in which a person actually acquires a colossal rack but then, due to ignorance or a lack of interest, fails to bring the deer to the attention of the hunting world. In such cases, the

> *"Like a talented pitcher who, for one reason or another, never gets to take the mound, many phenomenal bucks no doubt have faded from whitetail history without ever having actually entered it."*

deer seems not unlike a great athlete who plays out his stellar career without any sort of media coverage. Only those fans who attended his games would fully appreciate him for what he was and what he meant to his sport.

Fortunately, as this book, **Legendary Whitetails,** clearly shows, a number of enormous bucks have made it all the way through the gauntlet. They've not only been blessed with the right bloodlines but also have had the opportunity to develop fully. And finally—often against staggering odds—their racks have reached the hands of deer enthusiasts who have recognized them for the remarkable treasure they are.

Throughout this book, you'll notice that the featured bucks are accompanied by "score sheets," which are nothing more than charts of numbers giving the various measurements of each rack. To fully appreciate the sheer size of these bucks, it's imperative that you understand these numbers. So, let's take a quick look at what they mean.

The most universal antler-measuring system now in use was developed by the Boone and Crockett Club back in the early 1950s and is used for determining an overall score of a rack, for purposes of ranking it in the record book. Both hunter-taken trophies and specimens found dead are eligible for entry into the B&C records, provided the antlers are of sufficient score. The Pope and Young Club's record book is limited to animals taken in fair chase with bow and arrow,

At 333 7/8 points, the immense size of the world record non-typical shocked the whitetail world when it was found dead just outside St. Louis, Missouri, in 1981. Photo courtesy Missouri Department of Conservation.

but the same measuring system is used.

All whitetail racks can be placed in one of two categories—typical or non-typical. As the names imply, the typical category is for antlers with a fairly "standard" configuration, while non-typical racks deviate significantly from the norm. A typical rack has most, if not all, points originating from the tops of the main beams, rather than from other points or unusual positions on the beams. The non-typical category, conversely, includes racks that have a fair percentage of their growth being displayed in formations that don't fit the above definition of "typical" antlers.

All antler measurements are to the nearest 1/8 inch. Points of score equate directly to inches of measurement; thus, score is expressed in increments of 1/8 point. The gross score is the total of all measurements of the rack, while the net score is what's left after various deductions have been made. In all cases, typical and non-typical, deductions are made for asymmetry in the typical portion of the rack—that is, the difference between corresponding measurements from one antler to the other, such as the right brow tine vs. the left.

Abnormal (non-typical) points are accounted for in another way. In the typical category, the total length of all non-typical points is deducted from the score of the typical portion of the rack. However, in non-typicals, the total length of abnormal points is added to the score. Because a buck with abnormal points always will score higher as a non-typical than as a typical, the minimum score for inclusion in the B&C record book is somewhat higher for non-typicals than for typicals (195 vs. 170). The same rela-

tionship exists in the P&Y record categories as well, but due to the increased difficulty of hunting with archery equipment, the minimum scores for entry in that record book are far lower (150 for non-typicals, 125 for typicals).

The dream of taking a huge buck is what keeps most hunters tossing and turning the night before opening day. And, the ultimate fantasy is the thought of bagging a world record whitetail, a buck whose rack scores higher than any other. An animal of this stature is truly the Holy Grail of deer hunting.

Are such dreams ridiculous? Maybe not. While some hunters think the days of monster bucks are long gone, the evidence is clearly to the contrary. In fact, it's likely that even as you read these words, there's at least one living, breathing buck somewhere in North America that would be a new world record, if only somebody could get him. If you doubt it, then consider the stories of the current No. 1 typical and non-typical bucks— both of them deer that lived in the modern era of whitetail hunting, not in the fabled "good ol' days."

The World Record Typical 213 5/8 Points Saskatchewan, 1993

The specialized sport of trophy whitetail hunting was for years dominated by a single question: When will a new world record typical be taken? The 206 1/8-point Jim

Milo Hanson proudly displays his world record 12-pointer soon after the fateful hunt.
Photo by Gordon Whittington courtesy North American WHITETAIL.

Jordan Buck from Wisconsin, shot back in 1914, had been firmly seated on the throne for a number of years, and there hadn't even been that many serious threats to his No.1 ranking. On several occasions, other huge-framed typicals showed up but their net scores always fell short of Jordan's. It began to seem as though the Wisconsin buck was meant to reign forever.

Then, on November 23, 1993, along came a jolly Canadian deer hunter named Milo Hanson, and everything changed!

Prior to the end of the 1993 rifle season in Saskatchewan, had you mentioned Milo's name to anyone very far from the small town of Biggar, Saskatchewan, you almost certainly would have gotten a blank stare in return. But, any chance this farmer had of maintaining his anonymity disappeared at around 10:15 a.m. Eastern Standard Time on December 1 of that year, when the phone rang in my office at *North American WHITETAIL* magazine.

"Mr. Whittington, my name is Jim Wiebe," said the voice on the line, "and I've just measured a whitetail rack that will be a new world record in the typical category."

With that call, a brand new chapter in the annals of deer hunting history began to be written.

Jim went on to explain that the previous night he'd stretched a tape over the rack of a buck just shot by neighbor Milo Hanson, and in doing so, he had come up with an unofficial net of 215 5/8 typical points. That, of course, was the sort of score previously only dreamed about by whitetail fanatics. According to Jim, there was nothing controversial about the judgments he'd made in measuring the basic 12-point rack, so he was confident it would become No. 1. True, the rack would shrink a tad by the time B&C's mandatory 60-day drying period had passed, but there seemed to Jim no question that the final score would exceed Jordan's record by several inches.

Within 24 hours, *WHITETAIL* publisher Steve Vaughn and I had flown from Georgia to Saskatchewan and had seen Milo's deer with our own eyes. We stared at the rack for a long time, but we

"A long 79 years after Jim Jordan had downed his world record, Milo had shoved him aside with a monster that ultimately would be scored by a B&C judges' panel at 213 5/8 net points."

really didn't need to—the first glimpse convinced us that this was indeed the next world record. In fact, we were so sure of it that we never even bothered to take any measurements of our own!

I had the honor of penning the first-ever magazine feature on Milo's buck for the February 1994 issue of *WHITETAIL*, and it was an unforgettable experience. Visiting with Milo and his wife, Olive, and listening to the details of the hunt might not have been as exciting as actually shooting the deer myself, but at the time, it almost seemed that way. As I heard how the events had unfolded, it wasn't hard to imagine myself standing alongside Milo that historic morning scarcely more than a week earlier when the buck had run out of the bush.

During the summer of 1993, the big deer had been seen in the area around the Hanson farm, which lies several miles north of Biggar. But, Milo hadn't been among those lucky enough to glimpse the giant. In fact, as a busy farmer, he never even got a chance to scout for the buck before the November 15 rifle opener. That wasn't a huge handicap, though, because Milo and his buddies generally relied on the traditional method of "pushing bush" to cover ground and get deer moving.

It took a week of hard hunting, but their tactic paid off. Late on the morning of November 23, after the buck and two does had been jumped several times from small blocks of cover in this rolling farmland, Milo found himself in the right spot to make the fateful shot. His .308 Win.

Model 88 spoke as the buck turned away from him, and the animal crashed to earth—due at least in part to the fact that the bullet had passed through the body cavity and had smacked the right antler beam!

Had that antler broken off, Milo's buck would have been rendered unscorable and today he'd be just another sad footnote in whitetail history. But fortunately, while a small chunk of bone blew out of the impact area, the beam held. Shortly thereafter, Milo walked up to the buck and fired a finishing shot. A long 79 years after Jim Jordan had downed his world record, Milo had shoved him aside with a monster that ultimately would be scored by a B&C judges' panel at 213 5/8 net points.

To say this hunter overcame long odds in breaking the mark would be putting it mildly. For starters, he clearly was fortunate that such a trophy even existed on land he could hunt. Secondly, though many other hunters also were in the area, and a couple had even had shots at the deer, none had connected before Milo got his chance. Thirdly, on the morning of November 23, the buck ran out near Milo, rather than in front of someone else. And finally, even though that .308 bullet hit the right antler squarely, it didn't snap the beam. You could burn up a calculator trying to figure the probability of all of these events turning out exactly as they did.

Over the years, many phenomenal deer racks have been thrown away, or even left in the woods, simply because folks had no idea how significant they were. Thankfully, the Hanson Buck suffered no such indignities. A few days after the kill, local measurer Adam

Evashenko scored the rack unofficially at 214 points. Then, another local measurer, Bruce Kushner, took a crack at it and got a score of 214 6/8. The next day, Jim Wiebe stretched his own tape over the antlers, looked at the numbers, re-added them to make sure he wasn't crazy and then called me.

The rest, as they say, is history—and I'm thankful to have been a part of it.

The World Record Non-Typical 333 7/8 Points Missouri, 1981

When you dream of monster bucks, are they usually typicals? Or, does your mind prefer to conjure up visions of something a bit more gnarly? For those who favor the classic look of a high, wide and clean typical, the Hanson Buck is indeed a fantasy come to life. But, a lot of hunters would rather get a world-class non-typical because of the unique look and sheer amount of antler such racks have. For many whitetail "junkies" who feel the pangs of buck fever coming over them at the mere thought of this type of trophy, a buck from the outskirts of St. Louis, Missouri, is the standard by which all other deer are measured.

As was the case in the typical category, many observers long wondered if the world record non-typical could be beaten. The established mark was 286 points, and it belonged to a buck shot by Jeff Benson near Brady, Texas, all the way back in 1892. B&C had recognized the Texas deer as the clear No. 1 non-typical in the 1950s, when the scoring system was first implemented. Like the Jordan Buck, the Benson record had had few real challenges. Going into the fall of 1981, only one other buck (the 282-point non-typical shot in Iowa by Larry Raveling in 1973) had even cracked the 280-point mark. Many experts said flat out that they considered the 286-point mark unbreakable.

But, all such ideas regarding the upper limits of antler size became obsolete on November 11, 1981, when avid Missouri deer hunter Dave Beckman spotted an enormous whitetail lying dead near a highway only 20 miles from downtown St. Louis.

Dave reported the dead deer to Missouri Department of Conservation (MDOC) agent Mike Helland, who immediately recovered the animal and claimed it for the state. As you might imagine, Dave was less than thrilled with this announcement, as he had hoped to get to keep the antlers. But given the astounding size of the buck's rack, few observers were surprised to learn that in this case "finders" would be "weepers," not "keepers."

The 250-pound carcass was examined by MDOC personnel for clues as to what had claimed the great buck's life. There were no apparent bullet or arrow holes; nor could it be ascertained that he'd been hit by a vehicle. In the end, the monster's demise was simply chalked up to "natural causes." We'll probably never know for sure what killed him.

What we do know, however, is that news of this deer hit the hunting world like an atomic bomb, amazing even the experts. Never mind the old question of whether or not any whitetail antlers could outscore those of the Benson Buck; now, all that was left to ponder was exactly how far beyond the once-unthinkable 300-point mark this Missouri rack would go. The record books include thousands of great deer, and in most cases, the difference between one and the next in the rankings is far less than an inch. Now, it appeared certain that the gap between the old and new world records would be measurable in feet!

Indeed, after the drying period had ended, B&C measurer Dean Murphy of MDOC calculated the official net entry score at 325 3/8 points, a full 37 3/8 inches higher than the score of the Benson Buck. That was an amazing number— but it was to get even bigger. At the next B&C panel-measuring session in the spring of 1983, Dean and the other members of the judges' panel awarded the buck a final score of 333 7/8 points, only 1/8-inch short of being a full four feet greater than the score of Benson's Texas trophy.

If we judge deer by where they stand in the record book, the St. Louis and Hanson bucks are indeed the ultimate

> *"Many experts said flat out that they considered the 286-point mark unbreakable.*
> *But, all such ideas regarding the upper limits of antler size became obsolete on November 11, 1981, when Missouri hunter Dave Beckman spotted an enormous whitetail lying dead near a highway only 20 miles from downtown St. Louis."*

The St. Louis Buck (left) and the Hole-In-The-Horn Buck (right) are the only whitetails ever recorded to top 300 points, and the question of which is bigger is often raised. Photo courtesy Roger Selner.

whitetail trophies of all time, and any sportsman who plans on besting either of these giants obviously has his work cut out for him. Some hunters claim it won't ever happen. Maybe they're right. But then, plenty of folks also

"...the judges' panel awarded the buck a final score of 333 7/8 points, only 1/8-inch short of being a full four feet greater than the score of Benson's Texas trophy."

thought Babe Ruth's career mark of 714 home runs was untouchable...until a skinny kid named Henry Aaron proved them wrong. History keeps showing that no matter what the sport, even the legends' records are made to be broken.

Chapter One

THE DEL AUSTIN BUCK

279 7/8 NON-TYPICAL, NEBRASKA, 1962

The Saga Of "Mossy Horns" — World Record By Bow

BY DICK IDOL

Surprisingly few of the top whitetails in the record book were taken by serious hunters who knew of their presence and hounded them for any substantial amount of time. However, the story of the archery world record non-typical is perhaps history's most classic saga of a big buck hunt, even though the bowhunter who pursued the deer most fervently never got him.

This story begins back in the 1950s, along the Platte River south of Shelton, Nebraska, an area of open prairie and farmland that rolls for seemingly endless miles. Cover lies at the bottom of ravines and gullies, with most of the larger blocks of trees and brush being along the river and its major tributaries. Because of fertile soil in the bottoms, substantial crop fields also lie along this major waterway. The river is wide but fairly shallow, with much of the basin featuring islands of various shapes and sizes. Some are small, house-sized land masses, while others are more than a mile in length. Most are choked with heavy underbrush, especially willows, and some have large cottonwoods. The edge of the river itself is covered with the same types of trees and brush.

Photo by Ron Brown

Main Characteristics: Double drop tines at antler bases. A total of 39 points. 95 2/8" of abnormal points.

DEL AUSTIN, NEBRASKA, 1962

	Right Antler	Left Antler	Difference
Main Beam Length	27 7/8	28 1/8	2/8
1st Point Length	7 2/8	6 5/8	5/8
2nd Point Length	11 0/8	11 3/8	3/8
3rd Point Length	6 6/8	9 6/8	3 0/8
4th Point Length	7 2/8	8 2/8	1 0/8
5th Point Length	—	—	—
1st Circumference	6 5/8	6 6/8	1/8
2nd Circumference	5 3/8	5 2/8	1/8
3rd Circumference	5 0/8	5 2/8	2/8
4th Circumference	6 2/8	5 2/8	1 0/8
Total	83 3/8	86 5/8	6 6/8

MISCELLANEOUS STATS	
No. Of Points–Right	21
No. Of Points–Left	18
Total No. Of Points	39
Length Of Abnormals	95 2/8
Greatest Spread	29 5/8
Tip To Tip Spread	13 7/8
Inside Spread	21 3/8

FINAL TALLY	
Inside Spread	21 3/8
Right Antler	83 3/8
Left Antler	86 5/8
Gross Score	191 3/8
Difference	-6 6/8
Subtotal	184 5/8
Abnormals	+95 2/8
NET NON-TYPICAL SCORE	279 7/8

Back in 1958, rumors began to leak out about a giant buck with a "weird" rack that lived along the river and had been seen on the farm of Dan Thomas. This buck's most relentless pursuer turned out to be Al Dawson, who had heard the rumors. At that time, Al was 31 years old and lived in Hastings, about 30 miles southeast of Shelton. He'd recently started bowhunting, and he was so taken with it that he'd totally given up deer hunting with a gun.

Dan's farm was one Al especially enjoyed hunting, and one day during the 1958 season, he walked across a freshly cut corn field to look for deer sign. He'd stopped at a fence to look over an adjoining alfalfa field and the timbered river bottom beyond when he caught a glimpse of movement. Five or six deer had broken out of the timber and were heading straight for him.

In the lead was a tremendous buck. Not only was the deer huge, with a high, massive rack, but the antlers were also the most unusual Al had ever seen. "There were heavy, scraggly points, long and short, growing from the main beams in all directions," he said. "Strangest of all, he had these long prongs curving out and down on either side of his head, between eye and ear. They extended below his jaws, giving him an odd, lop-eared appearance."

It appeared the deer wanted to cross the fence on the trail where Al stood. The hunter had been caught in the open, so he risked taking a couple of steps backwards, sank to one knee and nocked an arrow.

By now, the non-typical and other deer had approached to within 50 or 60 yards, but suddenly, the buck swerved off to the side and cleared the fence 70 yards from Al. The monster then stopped broadside and looked directly at him. Al knew he wasn't going to come closer, and in the heat of the moment, he decided to take a shot. Not surprisingly, the arrow fell short, and the buck whirled around and led the entire herd back to the same wooded bottom from which they'd come.

Al retrieved his arrow and followed the huge tracks across the field for some distance. He knew there would be no hope for another shot, though, so he finally left the tracks and headed back to his car. That morning, the name "Mossy Horns" came to him, as it seemed to fit that irregular set of antlers. (Today, this name is still attached to the deer.) And that same morning, the bowhunter vowed he'd keep after that buck until the great trophy was his.

"In the lead was a tremendous buck. Not only was the deer huge, with a high, massive rack, but the antlers were also the most unusual Al had ever seen."

Al hunted the remainder of the bow season, which ended after Christmas, and had a half-dozen chances at lesser deer. But on each occasion, the thought of Mossy Horns kept him from shooting, as he had only a single deer tag. If he waited, there was always a chance. As it turned out, he did see the huge buck twice more that season but never got a shot.

During the 1958 season, Al had hunted the buck alone. But the following year, he'd be joined by a couple of fellow archery hunters. Gene Halloran, a retired farmer, and Charley Marlowe, a Hastings advertising executive and the only member of their Oregon Trail Bowhunters Club who'd killed a deer with a bow up to that time, also would become obsessed with the hunt for Mossy Horns.

By now, Dan Thomas had his own reasons for wanting the buck dead. A couple of years earlier, he'd planted 50 young spruce trees as a windbreak about 30 yards from his house and the big buck had taken it upon himself to destroy them. In one season, he'd killed all 50 with his antlers!

In the fall of 1959, Al, Charley and Gene built tree blinds in a half-dozen locations. In those days, portable tree stands were just being developed, so their ambush sites consisted of small platforms 10 to 20 feet off the ground. Despite their best efforts, most of the archery season passed without anyone even glimpsing the huge buck. By now, the old second-guessing game had begun. Charley shot a doe, ending his season. Al finally resigned himself to the possibility that the buck had moved to another area or was dead.

Still, he kept hunting. Then, late one November evening, he saw Mossy Horns about 150 yards away, following a slough. His movement was extremely slow and cautious, and it was clear that he'd pass well out of range. Several times he stopped at the edge of thickets to test the wind and listen for danger. This was the first time Al had seen him all year, and his rack appeared nearly identical to the one he'd worn the previous season.

Finally, Al decided he had nothing to lose by trying to stalk close enough for a shot. A strong wind was blowing from the deer to the archer, and there was enough brush that Al just might be able to stay out of sight.

For a half-mile, he moved along on the most careful stalk he'd ever made. Three times the buck stopped to thrash trees with his huge rack, and each time

At 281 4/8, the sheds from "Mossy Horns," probably dropped two years before Del Austin finally arrowed the buck, actually top the buck's official score of 279 7/8. Photo by Ron Brown.

the hunter crept closer. On two of those occasions, he was in bow range, but there was simply too much brush in the way. Finally, the buck paused at the edge of a thicket to work over another willow clump just 25 yards from Al. Two steps around a willow clump and the excited bowhunter would have an open shot. But just then, a dry twig broke underfoot and the buck was gone.

Al didn't see him again until the final evening of the season. As the tired hunter walked out of the river bottom at dusk, realizing the buck had eluded him for another season, he noticed a dark form standing in the open. Al finally made out the white throat patch and huge antlers as the buck stood calmly, watching him from just out of range. Then, the monster turned and disappeared into the gloom, drawing the season to a fitting close.

Al muttered, "Okay, Mossy. Next

year will be different."

During the summer of 1960, Dan saw the buck about once a month, each time near his old hangout in the river bottom. The same three hunters would once again do their best to get the deer, but now a fourth had joined the quest. A warehouse manager from Hastings, Del Austin was an enthusiastic convert to bowhunting and would hunt with the group for the next three seasons.

By the time the bow opener rolled around on September 10, all four archers knew Mossy Horns was still alive and well, and everyone felt confident they had his travel pattern down cold. Stands had been built long before the season. Al had the greatest faith in one stand he'd erected near the corner of a corn field, where it joined the river bottom. Here, he had found numerous fresh tracks which he felt could belong only to the non-typical, and he resolved to hunt this spot until the great buck showed.

For seven weeks, Al sat in the stand every chance he had. Over time, he grew progressively more impatient. Then, one cool afternoon toward the end of October, two bucks stepped into the corn field about 200 yards down the fence line from the stand. They were certainly not in the class of Mossy Horns, but they were good bucks, and it had been a long dry spell. Once the deer had disappeared into the standing corn, Al climbed down and began to stalk them.

The hunter had gone only about 70 yards when, for some reason, he looked

"Al finally made out the white throat patch and huge antlers as the buck stood calmly, watching him from just out of range. Then, the monster turned and disappeared into the gloom, drawing the season to a fitting close."

back toward his stand. Mossy Horns was standing under it! The gigantic buck stared toward Al, not sure what he was. Then the big deer caught human scent and was gone.

The following week, Charley was in his stand when four deer walked past. He, too, succumbed to temptation and arrowed a young buck, which promptly ran into the corn field and dropped. Charley had filled his deer tag for the year. But before he even could climb down, Mossy Horns stepped out of the brush and stood broadside at 30 yards! Finally, he blew and ran back toward the river.

Near the end of that same season, Al had yet another chance at the great buck. This time his wife, Velma, was sitting in another tree about 50 yards from where Al sat. It was getting dark, and Al was almost ready to depart. Then, the snap of a twig froze him as he looked into the brush. Mossy Horns was walking slowly toward him!

Al let the buck walk beneath his stand and a short distance beyond. The bowhunter was at full draw when the buck passed, and Al shot for the front shoulder. The arrow hit with a solid thud, and the deer instantly flinched and bolted. Beneath the stand where Velma sat, a woven-wire fence was nailed to the tree. As the buck crashed away, he hit the fence so hard that the tree shook, nearly knocking Velma from her perch. But, the buck kept going.

In the poor light, Al and Velma looked for blood but found none. Finally, they decided to wait a half-hour then return with a flashlight. Al still remembers that wait as being the longest 30 minutes of his life. When they returned, they found where the buck had crashed into the fence; they even recovered the feathered end of his arrow, but it had no blood on it. Even after further searching the next day, they encountered no trace of blood or the buck.

Al was haunted the rest of the season by concern that he might have killed the deer. Had he crawled into a thicket and died, or could he have been carried away by the river, never to be seen again? During the last week of the season, Al finally filled his tag with a big 8-pointer, which was his first deer with a bow and his third whitetail ever. The season ended with no more sightings of Mossy Horns.

During the summer of 1961, Dan didn't see the non-typical. This was unusual, as the farmer had observed the deer in each of the past three summers. Perhaps Al's arrow really had killed the buck, or maybe he'd simply died of old age. Judging from the size of his rack back in 1958, he now was presumed to be at least eight years old.

Later, one bitterly cold afternoon near the end of the '61 season, after the other hunters had given up, Al again was sitting in the stand from which he'd shot at Mossy Horns the previous year. Just before dark, he spotted a button buck making his way through the willows about 100 yards off. Following him was a large buck, and behind that buck was the one whitetail Al had expected never to see again — Mossy Horns!

Suddenly, the season took on an entirely new dimension. The giant moved as cautiously as ever while he worked his great rack through the willow bushes. His rack looked the same as before, and if anything, even bigger. Despite the cold, Al began to sweat.

Before dark, the two other bucks headed out into the field, but Mossy Horns remained in the willows. Then, a half-dozen does came out under Al's stand and began feeding. Soon, two younger bucks joined them, and all eight milled around near the stand until dark.

> *"The giant sheds had an 11-inch drop point off one base and one of 13 inches off the other base. Approximating the inside spread, the rack would have scored in excess of 281 non-typical points, easily making this buck just what Al had claimed — a Pope and Young world record."*

Mossy Horns finally entered the field just before dark, but he would come nowhere near Al's tree. It was as if he remembered the shot from a year earlier — and he probably did.

In the spring of 1962, Dan had the good fortune to find a matching pair of shed antlers from Mossy Horns, not far from where the guys had been hunting the buck. Now, it was clear that the buck was as big as Al had always claimed. (Charley was the only other hunter in Al's group who'd even seen the buck in four years!) Al had believed Mossy Horns was a new archery world record, but he'd had no proof. The evidence now was in hand.

The giant sheds had an 11-inch drop point off one base and one of 13 inches off the other base. Approximating the inside spread, the rack would have

Whitetail enthusiast Roger Selner (left) had to have help to display the two sets of sheds and the actual mounted head (right) of the archery world record non-typical. The Austin Buck has one of the best and most colorful stories leading up to the kill of any of the legendary bucks. Photo courtesy Roger Selner.

scored in excess of 281 non-typical points, easily making this buck just what Al had claimed—a Pope and Young world record.

As it turned out, the sheds probably were from the previous year—the '60 hunting season—which was the year Al thought he had hit the buck. Near the end of one of the long, clublike drop tines off the bases was what appeared to be a three-edged broadhead mark that had penetrated the antler about a half-inch! Instead of the arrow hitting the shoulder, as had been intended, it apparently had hit that antler tip! This would account for the buck's excessive crashing and hitting the fence, as he was temporarily stunned from the shock.

In 1962, Al's fifth season of hunting Mossy Horns, he decided to try a new tactic. For weeks in the summer, the archer cut trails through the heavy brush in places where he'd seen the buck most often. At the most likely crossings, he built tree stands. Then, starting a full month before bow season, Al kept away from the area to allow Mossy Horns time to get used to the changes. Once again, no one saw the old buck prior to the season.

At the time, Interstate 80 was being built on the north side of the bottoms where Mossy Horns lived. As a result, the Platte had been temporarily dammed upstream. One day early in the season, as Al walked the dry river bed, he found the fresh, unmistakable tracks of the non-typical. From the looks of it, the buck had been traveling to an alfalfa field. Al backtracked to a small island choked with willows, where he jumped the deer at close range. His rack looked just as big as ever.

During the next few days, Al was careful to keep away from the island and the primary trails the buck was using. One evening, while he sat in a tree where a runway crossed a big slough, several does walked under his stand, followed by an 8-point buck that stopped to rub his antlers on a bush. Mossy Horns showed up just after the smaller buck but eventually moved off without coming close enough for a shot. That same week, Al had one more distant look at him.

The following week the monster wasn't seen, so Al searched the dry river bed again to find out what he was doing. Here, the bowhunter found a trail the buck hadn't been using previously. Early bow season was drawing to an end, so Al decided to set up a new stand as a last-ditch effort. A nine-day rifle season would begin soon, and too many other local hunters knew of the legendary deer. He'd be lucky to survive the onslaught.

On Al's first evening in the new blind, an hour before dark, he saw the great buck slip out of the willows on an island and head his way. Mossy Horns crossed the dry channel and walked to within 15 yards of Al's stand. It appeared it was all over but the shot.

But as always before, something went wrong: The buck stopped in heavy brush. Finally, the buck circled the tree at 20 yards, but he never left the brush

"For some reason, Mossy Horns ran toward Del and stopped 20 yards from his tree, turning almost broadside. The archer drew his 45-pound Oneida recurve and drove a Bear Razorhead behind the shoulder of the deer, which promptly bolted."

for a clear shot. He locked up not 20 feet from Al's stand, where a fence came down to the river, but there was no chance to draw. After another 10 agonizing minutes, Mossy Horns jumped the fence and walked into the alfalfa field. He stopped broadside at 45 yards…and Al sent an arrow just over his back.

The last afternoon in October rolled around, and the early bow season was about to end. Al and Gene got to the bottoms early and chose their stands. Del and Charley left Hastings after work and hurried out to the farm to get in a last-minute hunt.

Originally, Del had planned to sit in one of Al's stands but now feared he wouldn't be able to find it quickly. So, he brought along a portable platform and placed it on a large island of thick brush and liberally sprinkled buck lure on the ground all around his tree.

Del stood on the platform until just before dark; then, as he was starting to get down, a loud crash from upwind caught his attention. It was hard to see antlers in the dim light and heavy cover, but the hunter could tell the buck was big. For some reason, he ran toward Del and stopped 20 yards from his tree, turning almost broadside. The archer drew his 45-pound Oneida recurve and drove a Bear Razorhead behind the shoulder of the deer, which promptly bolted.

Al and the other hunters waited for Del until an hour after dark, but still there was no sign of him. Finally, with flashlights, they headed toward the river and met him halfway. He related his story, noting that he wasn't sure if the deer he'd shot was Mossy Horns or another buck.

From the blood, it appeared Del had made a hard hit. After some searching, they found the broken arrow, which had been snapped off 10 inches above the head. For three hours, the hunters trailed the buck through slough grass and willow thickets until the blood and their flashlights were nearly gone. They decided it would be best to wait until daylight to continue the search.

The next morning, within 100 yards of where they had stopped the previous evening, they found the buck lying dead in a clump of willows. He was indeed Mossy Horns! It was a bittersweet moment for Al Dawson. The five-year quest had ended with someone else taking "his" buck. On the other hand, one of his buddies had been fortunate, and that was reason enough to celebrate.

Mossy Horns was showing signs of age. He had no fat on his body, and his loins were sunken. Even so, he dressed 240 pounds, and

"At the time, this buck was the second largest non-typical in the world (behind only the 286-point Jeff Benson Buck from Texas), and Mossy Horns was far and away the new world record by bow."

Al felt sure he would have been 60 pounds heavier during earlier years. The rack wasn't quite as massive as it had been earlier, but it still scored 279 7/8 points when measured by P&Y's Glenn St. Charles. At the time, this buck was the second largest non-typical in the world (behind only the 286-point Jeff Benson Buck from Texas), and Mossy Horns was far and away the new world record by bow. This buck is indeed a fitting archery world record, and even after all of these years, he's faced no serious challenges to that title.

Perhaps the most interesting aspect of this story is what it tells us about the lifestyle of a monster buck. Rarely is there any account through which we can get to know a deer of this caliber and see how he avoids dangers time after time. Despite being subjected to serious hunting pressure, this giant came within minutes, perhaps seconds, that fateful afternoon of perhaps surviving to die of old age. Can you imagine how seldom Mossy Horns would have been seen by casual hunters who didn't know he even existed?

Chapter Two

THE KEN BARCUS BUCK

225 1/8 NON-TYPICAL, MISSOURI, 1982

Lightning Can Strike Twice In The Same Spot

BY LES DAVENPORT

Who says lightning never strikes twice in the same spot? Certainly not Ken Barcus! The Missouri hunter took the featured 225 1/8-inch buck and one decade later to the day harvested a second Boone and Crockett non-typical scoring 233 1/8!

Missouri recorded 24 non-typicals by the printing of Boone and Crockett's 10th Edition. At 333 7/8, the phenomenal 44-pointer known as the "St. Louis Buck" ranks tops in the world. The oldest Missouri entry fell to Vernon Sower in 1953. Vernon's Chariton County whitetail netted 203 5/8.

The odds of any hunter harvesting a B&C non-typical are remote, even in a great whitetail state like Missouri. How remote? If Missouri's B&C entries by hunters were divided by the state's approximated total deer harvest since the inaugural Sower buck of 1953, chances of scoring a non-typical are worse than a quarter-million to one! Such insurmountable odds make the Ken Barcus story a veritable miracle.

Saturday, opening day of Missouri's firearm season in 1982 found Ken Barcus

KEN BARCUS, MISSOURI, 1982

	Right Antler	Left Antler	Difference
Main Beam Length	30 6/8	31 0/8	2/8
1st Point Length	9 2/8	9 1/8	1/8
2nd Point Length	8 7/8	8 3/8	4/8
3rd Point Length	10 4/8	10 3/8	1/8
4th Point Length	9 3/8	9 2/8	1/8
5th Point Length	1 7/8	6 0/8	4 1/8
1st Circumference	5 6/8	5 5/8	1/8
2nd Circumference	5 0/8	5 0/8	–
3rd Circumference	5 0/8	5 5/8	5/8
4th Circumference	5 0/8	5 0/8	–
Total	**91 3/8**	**95 3/8**	**6 0/8**

Main Characteristics: Long main beams, both over 30". Net typical frame of 204 2/8. Makes record book as both a typical and non-typical.

MISCELLANEOUS STATS	
No. Of Points–Right	8
No. Of Points–Left	10
Total No. Of Points	18
Length Of Abnormals	20 7/8
Greatest Spread	27 0/8
Tip To Tip Spread	21 0/8
Inside Spread	23 4/8

FINAL TALLY	
Inside Spread	23 4/8
Right Antler	91 3/8
Left Antler	95 3/8
Gross Score	210 2/8
Difference	-6 0/8
Subtotal	204 2/8
Abnormals	+20 7/8
NET NON-TYPICAL SCORE	225 1/8

returning home with an unfilled permit. Ten deer had passed him, but not one carried horns. The early Sunday morning hunt proved equally antlerless.

Things changed quickly, however, when Ken and his neighbor switched hunting spots during mid-morning on Sunday. They had just left their pickup and headed afield when a huge buck bounded along a tree line almost directly at them. The deer had obviously been chased from a hiding place by another hunter.

Ken took aim and triggered his Winchester .243 Model 70. A heart shot dropped Missouri's new No. 2 non-typical. The 225 1/8-inch Nodaway County whitetail sported a 5x6 basic frame and nine abnormal points. Only two area farmers had ever seen the wide-antlered buck before that fateful Sunday.

The 30 6/8 and 31-inch main beams of Ken's 4 1/2-year-old deer spanned a greatest spread of 27 inches. As per 10th Edition records, only three non-typical whitetails average longer main beams. In

1985, Duane R. Linscott bumped the Barcus Buck to No. 3 in the Missouri standings by tagging a 259 5/8-inch 27-pointer in Chariton County.

Ken had two new hunting partners by opening day of the 1992 hunting season, wife Marcia and 14-year-old son, Scott. As a 22-year veteran of the sport, Ken had worked hard at instructing his companions so they might avoid some of the frustrations that confronted him as a self-taught whitetail hunter.

A combination of stand hunting and deer drives had always produced well for Ken in past years. Using these tactics during the first day and a half in 1992 failed to put antlers in Barcus crosshairs. But, Ken knew it was just a matter of time before one of the drives would flush a "shooter."

The Barcus family hunted 1,000 acres that was either owned or rented by Ken's father, a farmer. Terrain on this property provided ideal whitetail habitat—vast acreage of row crops intermixed with large and small tracts of timber, creeks and overgrown pastures. Only eight hunters enjoyed permission to pursue deer on the Barcus acreage, a situation favoring buck longevity and size.

Setting up and executing one last drive would finish out Sunday afternoon, the second day of Missouri's eight-day deer season. Ken chose to push a brush-choked thicket known for housing pressured bucks. This tract lay three miles from where Ken had scored on his buck in 1982.

Marcia posted where deer might exit in a low area. Scott was instructed to start walking the thicket's core after giving Ken time to reach an opposing periphery.

Action came quickly. Two does and two bucks erupted from their beds. One of the bucks looked more like an elk than a whitetail. Only after determining that conditions favored the safety of all hunters did Ken fire a Remington .270 Model 700 at the departing buck. He watched the enormous whitetail buck continue cross-country to another span of timber.

The target never winced and no blood marked the deer's tracks, which indicated a miss to Ken. "No way we'll ever see that big fella again," father told son.

Ken had long learned, however, that Lady Luck rarely knocked on the door of a defeatist. He reorganized Team Barcus and initiated one last drive on the suspect woodlot.

Not long into the drive, Scott spotted the elk-like buck break from heavy cover and bound across open ground. He fired twice but led the fleeing animal by too great a margin. Scott's shots turned the deer toward his father. One shot from Ken's .270 dropped the buck, halting its escape. A second shot for good measure absolved needless suffering.

The second B&C non-typical taken by the Missouri hunter carried 27 score-able points. Seven drop tines, three from the right beam and four off the left, highlighted the uniqueness of this great set of antlers. The buck officially netted 233 1/8 inches.

No man has ever taken two non-typicals averaging more inches than the bucks killed by Ken Barcus. "I was lucky," said Ken during an interview. "It was a matter of being at the right place at the right time."

"Amen" to that …twice!

Chapter Three

THE
BRIAN BICE BUCK

256 1/8 NON-TYPICAL, ILLINOIS, 1992

A Story Of Perseverence And A Cool Hand

BY LES DAVENPORT

Going into the fall of 1992, Illinois hunters were anticipating the best deer season in the state's history. Seemingly, everybody and his brother knew the whereabouts of a living Boone and Crockett buck. But with the rut approaching, those rosy predictions were forgotten when Mother Nature altered the playing field by deluging this part of the Midwest with its wettest November on record. Many fair-weather whitetailers simply gave up their quest for venison, opting instead for warm quarters and dry underwear. To make matters worse, unpicked corn fields stretched for mile after mile, offering bucks even more hideouts than usual. But, 28-year-old McDonough County resident Brian Bice persevered, and it paid big dividends.

He and friend Danny Vanbrooker were a bit distraught as they ate breakfast as DJ's Restaurant in Colchester before dawn on Sunday, November 22. They had not seen anything resembling a wallhanger buck during the cold, windy, rainy weather of the previous two days. It was now the third and final day of the first shotgun season, and the forecast called for still more chilly rain. Brian and Danny's spirits were low, but they knew some big bucks inhabited the area they hunted. If only the weather

Brian Bice, Illinois, 1992

Main Characteristics: G-2 on left side is 18 5/8" long. Tines curve forward, giving a "wind-swept" appearance.

	Right Antler	Left Antler	Difference
Main Beam Length	30 1/8	29 0/8	1 1/8
1st Point Length	9 1/8	8 0/8	1 1/8
2nd Point Length	14 6/8	18 5/8	3 7/8
3rd Point Length	13 5/8	11 6/8	1 7/8
4th Point Length	3 2/8	6 7/8	3 5/8
5th Point Length	–	–	–
1st Circumference	5 3/8	5 5/8	2/8
2nd Circumference	4 6/8	4 7/8	1/8
3rd Circumference	4 2/8	4 2/8	–
4th Circumference	3 3/8	3 7/8	4/8
Total	**88 5/8**	**92 7/8**	**12 4/8**

Miscellaneous Stats	
No. Of Points–Right	11
No. Of Points–Left	16
Total No. Of Points	27
Length Of Abnormals	65 2/8
Greatest Spread	24 0/8
Tip To Tip Spread	13 7/8
Inside Spread	21 7/8

Final Tally	
Inside Spread	21 7/8
Right Antler	88 5/8
Left Antler	92 7/8
Gross Score	**203 3/8**
Difference	-12 4/8
Subtotal	**190 7/8**
Abnormals	+65 2/8
Net Non-Typical Score	**256 1/8**

would cooperate…

The friends relished their final sips of hot coffee, then reluctantly left the comfort of the cafe. Neither was looking forward to becoming soaked to the bone for the third day in a row, but they knew they weren't likely to tag out while sitting in that restaurant.

Predicting that deer likely would not be moving on their own in the steady downpour, the hunters opted to sit it out in Danny's truck for a while, hoping for some kind of break in the weather. No

dice. Heavy rain continued for the duration of the morning, eating up valuable hunting time. Finally, Brian and Danny couldn't wait any longer. Separate obligations were calling them back to town. Disappointed, they bid each other farewell until they could rendezvous once again for the four-day slug season coming up less than two weeks later.

Brian's lunch commitment wrapped up earlier than he'd expected, which afforded him enough daylight to retrieve the 4-wheel ATV he'd left at the hunting property. It was still nasty out, but upon reaching the hunting area, he decided to try still-hunting a series of brushy draws before darkness arrived. Winchester 12 gauge in hand, he headed for the muddy outback.

The hunter tiptoed along the edges of several known bedding areas, but only one doe was spotted. Again feeling a bit morose, Brian retreated from the timber and loaded the ATV into the truck, all the while struggling with whether or not to abandon the hunt. One more go at it, he finally decided.

The landowner had told him that deer sometimes bedded in a narrow strip of scrub trees and tall grass paralleling the access road. Brian would still-hunt the strip then, if nothing happened, call it quits. Focused on the task ahead and the soon-to-be warmth of home, he began his final quest.

"The deer has a huge 5x5 typical frame, including a left G-2 tine that, at 18 5/8 inches, is among the longest on record. You sometimes see back tines that long on mule deer but virtually never on whitetails!"

Easing along the strip of cover, Brian spotted a flash of white not far into the underbrush. He stopped momentarily but could not pick up the source of movement through the steady drizzle. Then, advancing slightly, he noticed "steam" rising from the grass. Antler tips pivoted, revealing the head and billowing nostrils of a huge buck bedded in the thick growth!

Brian froze in place, assessing the situation and trying to figure out what to do. Finally, the hunter decided to attempt a shot to drop the buck where he lay. Vegetation wet with rain dampened the roar of the slug gun; the buck jumped to his feet and disappeared in the brush.

Brian hurried to the spot and, only yards from his bed, found the deer hit in the lungs. Ironically, the rain that had made slug season so miserable for trophy hunters also had taken the edge away from this 4 1/2-year-old, 27-point non-typical.

The Bice Buck, which had an estimated live weight of 250 pounds, officially scores 256 1/8 B&C points, making him the new all-time No. 2 non-typical in Illinois. Only Richard Paul's 267 3/8-point buck from Peoria County, taken in 1983, outscores this one. Brian's trophy primarily depends on tremendous tine length, rather than mass, to reach his final score. The deer has a huge 5x5 typical frame, including a left G-2 tine that, at 18 5/8 inches, is among the longest on record. You sometimes see back tines that long on mule deer but virtually never on whitetails!

In retrospect, I think it's fair to claim that most hunters would have failed in their efforts to take the gigantic buck Brian harvested that soggy Sunday in 1992. First, few would have kept plugging in that kind of weather. Many of those who would have gone afield might have failed to see that buck in the brush. Then, how many hunters would have had the presence of mind to calmly shoot him as he lay partially obscured in his bed? Brian not only worked hard for his chance, but he kept his composure under pressure and made that shot count. And when it's all said and done, that's often how thin the line between success and failure really is.

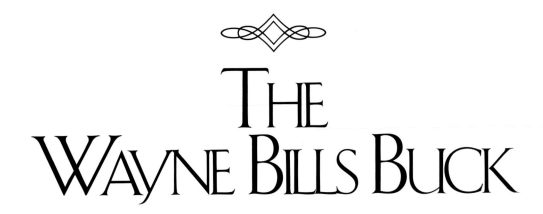

Chapter Four

THE WAYNE BILLS BUCK

201 4/8 TYPICAL, IOWA, 1974

Just A "What If"
Away From No. 1

BY DICK IDOL

In the late 1980s and early '90s, there was no shortage of rumors about "new" world record typical whitetails. Jim Jordan's long-standing world record from Wisconsin, with a net Boone and Crockett score of 206 1/8 points, was still the target to shoot for, but tales of bigger typicals abounded.

As most serious hunters know, until Milo Hanson's 1993 Saskatchewan buck (final score 213 5/8 points) was taken, all of these "world record" rumors proved to be no more than wishful thinking. But in 1992, a very real buck came onto the scene that refueled the hope that a new world record typical could show up at any time. While he didn't actually pose a serious threat to the Jordan Buck's No. 1 position, had a couple of very possible "what ifs" been so, the annals of deer hunting history might have told a different story.

Shot in Iowa in 1974, this buck was known to the "in" crowd of the whitetail fraternity for many years before he was officially entered into the B&C record book. However, the vast majority of hunters knew nothing of the buck prior to his appear-

Wayne Bills, Iowa, 1974

	Right Antler	Left Antler	Difference
Main Beam Length	27 5/8	29 1/8	1 4/8
1st Point Length	7 1/8	4 7/8	2 2/8
2nd Point Length	14 4/8	13 2/8	1 2/8
3rd Point Length	14 0/8	13 6/8	2/8
4th Point Length	10 5/8	12 5/8	2 0/8
5th Point Length	–	–	–
1st Circumference	5 5/8	5 2/8	3/8
2nd Circumference	5 1/8	5 2/8	1/8
3rd Circumference	5 4/8	5 2/8	2/8
4th Circumference	5 1/8	5 2/8	1/8
Total	**95 2/8**	**94 5/8**	**8 1/8**

Main Characteristics: If the left brow tine were not broken, this buck would probably have scored 206. He is still one of the all-time greats.

Miscellaneous Stats	
No. Of Points–Right	6
No. Of Points–Left	6
Total No. Of Points	12
Length Of Abnormals	3 2/8
Greatest Spread	25 2/8
Tip To Tip Spread	20 5/8
Inside Spread	23 0/8

Final Tally	
Inside Spread	23 0/8
Right Antler	95 2/8
Left Antler	94 5/8
Gross Score	**212 7/8**
Difference	-8 1/8
Subtotal	204 6/8
Abnormals	-3 2/8
Net Typical Score	**201 4/8**

ance at the B&C Awards Program in Milwaukee in 1992, where his panel-confirmed net score of 201 4/8 points was announced. Overnight, the deer was propelled onto the elite list of typicals officially in the book at over 200 points.

It doesn't take long to tell the story of the hunt for this monster. In the fall of 1974, Wayne Bills was asked by some friends to go on a deer hunt. He was relatively new to the sport; in fact, he had never shot a deer. Figuring a shotgun hunt would be a lot of fun, he agreed to take part in the hunt, which was to occur in Hamilton County about 70 miles north of Des Moines.

"Perhaps the most fascinating aspect of this buck is that he probably was a 'walking world record' in the weeks before he was shot. The reason I make this claim is that the left brow tine has a large piece missing off the end, badly hurting the final score."

In Iowa, "party" hunting is both legal and popular. Large groups commonly get together and conduct deer drives, with each hunter carrying a tag. If a hunter is fortunate enough to shoot more than one deer, he can tag the extra one with another party member's unfilled tag. The only restriction is that the total number of deer taken can't exceed the number of tags.

Not long into this particular hunt, Wayne heard several shots coming from behind him. He looked back in time to see a huge buck running down an open draw between two hills. The hunter moved into position and drew a bead on the rapidly moving buck, which was still some distance away. Not having enough experience to realize that the opportunity for a clean kill at that range was marginal at best, Wayne steadied his shotgun and fired. The hunter was somewhat sur-

prised to see the buck go down immediately. To his credit, Wayne didn't just stand there and hope the shot was fatal; he hurried over to where the deer was lying, just in time to see him try to get to his feet. A final shot ended it.

At the time, Wayne knew he'd shot a big buck, but he didn't realize just how big. Over the next few weeks, the response from taxidermists, other hunters, friends, etc., made him realize that the deer was much more noteworthy than he'd even imagined. Eventually, the rack was scored at 199 5/8 typical points, making it the state record. However, that score never was entered into B&C, which explains why the rack remained unknown to many trophy hunters for so long.

In time, collector Larry Huffman acquired the antlers, and in 1991, he had them measured again—this time by Dave Boland of Minnesota, one of the top scorers for B&C. Dave gave the head an entry score of 201 4/8 typical points as a basic 5x5 typical, and Larry submitted the application to B&C. That entry score was confirmed by the judges' panel in Milwaukee.

Perhaps the most fascinating aspect of this buck is that he probably was a "walking world record" in the weeks before he was shot. The reason I make this claim is that the left brow tine has a large piece missing off the end, badly hurting the final score. The portion that remains is 4 7/8 inches in length. The right brow, by contrast, is unbroken and measures 7 1/8 inches. Because of deductions for asymmetry, the buck gets a total of 9 6/8 inches (by doubling the shorter measurement) as his net total for the two brow points combined. The left brow, however, appears to have been at least as long as the right one originally, judging from the tine's diameter at the break. So, it seems safe to assume that the Bills Buck would have scored much better had the brow tine not been damaged. Had that tine been at least as long as its mate, the buck would have received another 4 4/8 inches of credit on his net score (double the current 2 2/8 inches of difference), which would have made his net score 206 points even. That, of course, would have put him just 1/8 inch below the James Jordan Buck.

It's unclear exactly how the brow tine was damaged. However, the break apparently was fresh at the time the deer was shot, because it doesn't look to have been smoothed by rubbing. It's quite possible that during all of that shooting before the buck reached Wayne, somebody shot the tip of the tine off. (Wayne's first shot hit the deer on the bridge of the nose.)

Another "what if" to consider when discussing this buck's run at the record is the fact that he was officially scored nearly two decades after he was shot. Although B&C's mandatory drying period for trophies is 60 days, shrinkage certainly doesn't end then. It's safe to assume that with the extra portion of the left brow tine, and with the buck being scored within the first year after he was shot, the deer easily could have scored as much as one to three points higher than he did when officially measured. This would have given him a final score of around 207 to 209, making him the world record for many years.

The awesome side view of a near world record buck… the stuff of dreams! Photo by Dick Idol.

Of course, you could make the same argument that the Jordan Buck (killed in 1914) and the John Breen Buck (a 202 typical shot in Minnesota in 1918) also would have scored higher than they do today had they been scored soon after they were taken. They certainly would have, but the B&C scoring system wasn't even formulated until 1950. So, there's no way these two giants could have been scored 60 days after they were taken. But, Wayne's buck could have been. Of course, that broken brow tine renders moot the question of whether or not he was a "world record"

"The symmetry of the rack is reflected in the fact that there is a total difference of only 8 1/8 inches between the two antlers—2 2/8 of which is a result of the broken brow tine alone."

on the hoof. But, it makes for interesting speculation.

The symmetry of the rack is reflected in the fact that there is a total difference of only 8 1/8 inches between the two antlers—2 2/8 of which is a result of the broken brow tine alone. The "natural" difference from one antler to the other appears to have been only 5 7/8 inches, an incredibly small amount for a rack that grosses 212 7/8 typical. As is, the typical frame score of 204 6/8 (before 3 2/8 inches of abnormal deductions) is still most impressive, particularly for a 5x5 with a broken point!

Chapter Five

THE JOHN BLAQUIERE BUCK

233 2/8 NON-TYPICAL, SASKATCHEWAN, 1981

A Miracle Shot In The Big Bush

BY GREG MILLER

I t was late in the day on November 21, 1981. A deer hunter by the name of John Blaquiere was slowly making his way along a cutline that dissected a large tract of bush near Meadow Lake, Saskatchewan. Walking through the thick cover off to John's right were two members of his hunting party. Two other party members waited in ambush at the far end of the cover, hoping the men walking through the bush would move a buck their way.

The drive was about half completed when John glimpsed a flicker of movement some distance ahead of him on the cutline. To his surprise, a deer had walked out of the cover on the opposite side of the cutline and was going to enter the piece of bush his party was driving.

"I brought my rifle up and looked through the scope at the deer," John remembered. "I could see right away that it was a real big buck. The range had to be close to 400 yards, but I decided to shoot anyway. I put the crosshairs on the top of his back and touched off a shot. When I recovered from the recoil, the buck was gone."

John, who lives in Edam, Saskatchewan, had the good fortune to be hunting that particular day with four lifelong residents of the Meadow Lake area. One of those individuals just happened to be a man by the name of Art Schreiner.

"Art was a wonderful person. He also was one of the best hunters I've ever met,"

Main Characteristics: Picturesque non-typical with drop tine on right side.

JOHN BLAQUIERE, SASKATCHEWAN, 1981

	Right Antler	Left Antler	Difference
Main Beam Length	30 0/8	28 5/8	1 3/8
1st Point Length	5 3/8	8 2/8	2 7/8
2nd Point Length	11 3/8	10 5/8	6/8
3rd Point Length	11 1/8	11 6/8	5/8
4th Point Length	7 2/8	4 1/8	3 1/8
5th Point Length	–	–	–
1st Circumference	5 2/8	5 1/8	1/8
2nd Circumference	4 6/8	4 4/8	2/8
3rd Circumference	5 1/8	5 3/8	2/8
4th Circumference	5 0/8	4 6/8	2/8
Total	**85 2/8**	**83 1/8**	**9 5/8**

MISCELLANEOUS STATS	
No. Of Points–Right	12
No. Of Points–Left	13
Total No. Of Points	25
Length Of Abnormals	52 1/8
Greatest Spread	28 1/8
Tip To Tip Spread	10 3/8
Inside Spread	22 3/8

FINAL TALLY	
Inside Spread	22 3/8
Right Antler	85 2/8
Left Antler	83 1/8
Gross Score	190 6/8
Difference	-9 5/8
Subtotal	181 1/8
Abnormals	+52 1/8
NET NON-TYPICAL SCORE	233 2/8

John said. "If you wanted to hunt moose, he knew just where to look. If you wanted to hunt deer, he knew exactly which patches of bush to check. He always knew where you could find game."

Along with having an intimate knowledge of the area and the wild animals living there, Art also was blessed with an endless supply of energy.

"Art was one of those guys who could walk all day and never tire out," John added. "He seemed to always have as much enthusiasm at the end of the day as

he did at the beginning. His enthusiasm inspired the rest of us to keep going even when we had run out of energy."

While there is a good deal of open cropland around Meadow Lake, there also are expansive tracts of bush, some of which go for miles without being dissected by a road. Of course, this situation is conducive to the production of trophy whitetails. Art and John, as well as the rest of the hunting party, knew this and felt confident that they would encounter something big when they took to the bush that fateful day.

As it worked out, conditions were ideal for a hunt. About a half-foot of snow lay on the ground, and the temperature was around the freezing mark. But even with the great conditions, the group of hunters had pushed the bush all day without rousting a big buck. The only thing they had to show for their efforts was one small buck shot near midday.

Then, late in the day, the men were down to their last drive. As John remembers, "I was the oldest member of the group and no doubt the most tired after our all-day hunt. For that reason, Art suggested that I take the easiest route. I decided to walk a cutline that ran along one side of the piece of cover we were going to push. I was supposed to keep an eye out for any bucks that might try to slip out the side of the drive."

That's just what John was doing when the monster buck mentioned at the beginning of this story stepped out onto the cutline.

"At first, I thought I'd missed the buck. Then, as I got closer, I could see him laying on his back with all four feet sticking in the air," John said. "The two guys walking in the bush next to me came out to the cutline, and we went running toward the buck. By the time we got there, he had dragged himself into the thick brush. We saw that the bullet from my .30-06 had broken the his back.

"One of the hunters with me wanted to finish off the buck with a shot to the head, but because of the thick underbrush, I was afraid he'd end up shooting off part of the rack." John continued. "I was able to talk him out of doing that, and the big buck quickly expired on his own. Afterwards, I paced off the distance

of my shot and found it was just under 420 yards. I know it was a long ways."

All the men in the group has seen huge bucks in the past, but none equaled this deer. A preliminary count put the number of points at 24, including a short drop tine toward the end of the left main beam and another much longer drop tine on the right beam. These two drops, along with a huge typical frame, make this a truly impressive set of antlers.

John's buck was officially measured sometime later. The final non-typical score came in at 233 2/8, enabling John to win a number of local big buck contests. Eventually, his buck was recognized as being the largest taken in the entire province during the 1981 season.

The high-scoring non-typical is helped along by lengthy main beams of 30 and 28 5/8 inches and some fairly hefty circumference totals, including bases of 5 2/8 and 5 1/8 inches. The greatest spread of the rack is an impressive 28 1/8 inches, while the inside spread tapes out at 22 3/8 inches. Also, the official score sheet shows that the rack actually possesses 25 scorable points, 12 on the right beam and 13 on the left.

"I've hunted deer for more than 40 years, and I've taken my share of bucks during that time. But, none mean as much to me as this one," John stated. "And, I don't feel that way just because the non-typical happens to be the largest deer I've ever shot. Rather, it's because I was hunting with Art Schreiner at the time. I really feel blessed, both for having him as a friend and for getting the opportunity to hunt with him."

Tragically, Art died of cancer a few years after John shot his big non-typical. He was 39 years old.

Chapter Six

THE JOHN BREEN BUCK

202 TYPICAL, MINNESOTA, 1918

*Former No. 1
And Still One
Of The Greatest*

BY DUNCAN DOBIE

The John Breen Buck, shot in northern Minnesota in 1918, is considered by many whitetail experts to be the greatest typical ever, despite the fact that at 202 net B&C points he's several notches down the list from No. 1. This isn't an attempt to take anything away from the incredible trophies that outscore him, but few other typicals can approach this buck's "shock value."

Back in 1903, John took a job as a store clerk in the northern Minnesota town of Bemidji. At that time, a vast area of logged-over woods lay between there and the Canadian border 100 miles to the north. Transportation in the region was difficult, and the use of a horse and buggy was still common. From Bemidji, a railroad ran northeastward all the way to the border town of International Falls. Some 30 miles from Bemidji, the tracks went through the small town of Funkley in Beltrami County. And, that's where whitetail history was made.

"People who lived north of Bemidji liked to catch the train and ride it into town to do their shopping," said Ray, John's youngest son. "In those days, you could flag the train down anywhere along its route and ride it for two cents a mile. For a lot of

JOHN BREEN, MINNESOTA, 1918

	Right Antler	Left Antler	Difference
Main Beam Length	31 2/8	31 0/8	2/8
1st Point Length	5 6/8	6 3/8	5/8
2nd Point Length	12 4/8	11 6/8	6/8
3rd Point Length	12 4/8	13 2/8	6/8
4th Point Length	9 4/8	11 3/8	1 7/8
5th Point Length	–	–	–
1st Circumference	5 7/8	6 0/8	1/8
2nd Circumference	5 6/8	5 5/8	1/8
3rd Circumference	6 1/8	6 1/8	–
4th Circumference	5 3/8	5 2/8	1/8
Total	**94 5/8**	**96 6/8**	**4 5/8**

Main Characteristics: Great height, spread and mass. Tremendous main beam length of 31 2/8" and 31 0/8". One of the best ever.

MISCELLANEOUS STATS

No. Of Points–Right	8
No. Of Points–Left	8
Total No. Of Points	16
Length Of Abnormals	8 3/8
Greatest Spread	26 7/8
Tip To Tip Spread	20 6/8
Inside Spread	23 5/8

FINAL TALLY

Inside Spread	23 5/8
Right Antler	94 5/8
Left Antler	96 6/8
Gross Score	215 0/8
Difference	-4 5/8
Subtotal	210 3/8
Abnormals	-8 3/8
NET TYPICAL SCORE	202 0/8

people, it was a real treat.

"One of Dad's customers, Knute Week, lived up near Funkley, at a flagstop place known as Hopt. He would come into Bemidji every so often to do his shopping. Week had access to some good deer hunting land up near Funkley, and he invited Dad to go up and hunt with him," Ray recalled.

One cold day in November 1918, while two of his sons were overseas fighting in World War I, John grabbed his rifle and gear and hopped aboard the train for Funkley. When he returned home a day or two later, he had with him a deer so large that even back then it created quite a stir.

"I still can remember when he brought it home," said Ray, who was 12 at the time. "He had quite a time getting it back to the house. He had to bring it down to Bemidji by train; then he had to get a horse and wagon to transport it from the depot to our house. The story that I always heard was that he was on his stand with his .30/30 rifle when a bunch of deer came by. Several does were being chased by a buck. He raised

This view from the buck's left side reveals both the great size and the symmetry of his basic 10-point frame. It's hard to imagine a more impressive typical. Photo by Dick Idol courtesy North American WHITETAIL.

his rifle and started to shoot the buck. All of a sudden, he saw this great rack of horns coming through the woods, so he took aim and shot this big buck instead.

"When he got the buck home, everybody came by to see it. A lot of people made a big fuss over it. The rack was so big that even in those days everybody knew that it was something special. The rack was so wide that we had a hard time getting it through the front door of the house.

"Dad knew his buck was really unusual," Ray added, "and he was awfully proud of it. After much deliberation, he decided to have it mounted. He sent the antlers over to a taxidermist in Duluth—a man named Story. Mr. Story took one look at those antlers and offered him $50 cash for them. Now, $50 was a lot of money back in those days, probably equal to about half a month's wages. Dad turned him down flat. That deer meant too much to him.

At the 1950 B&C Awards Banquet, John Breen's sons, Ray (left) and Art, proudly display their father's buck and the certificate that recognizes it as the world record typical. Photo courtesy the Breen family.

"It seemed like we ate on that old buck for weeks," Ray added, "and he was one tough old boy. The deer was thin and gaunt when Dad brought him home, despite the size of his antlers. He was a big-bodied deer, and I remember people saying that he weighed well over 200 pounds. Dad tried to give away some of the meat, but it was so tough that nobody wanted it."

John died in 1947 at the age of 81. Several years later, B&C introduced its new scoring system, and at the urging of friends, the family decided to have the head officially measured. With an unprecedented net typical score of 202 points, the Breen Buck immediately

became the world record typical, even though he suffered heavy deductions for non-typical points. The Breen Buck held the record until 1964, when the James Jordan Buck was recognized as a new No. 1 typical.

During the late 1960s, an antler collector from the East Coast wrote the Breen family and asked if they wanted to sell the rack.

"His name was Dr. Chuck Arnold, a dentist in Boston," Ray recalled. "He wasn't sure whether we spoke English or not, so he wrote to us in both French and English. He said he collected antlers, and he offered us $1,000 for the rack. After talking it over, we decided not to take his offer because we didn't want the antlers to leave northern Minnesota. After all, Dad's trophy was Minnesota's largest typical whitetail of all time (a position the deer still holds today), and we felt it should remain in the state. However, by this time, the old mount was beginning to show its age. For a while, we let it hang in a local store, but most of the time, it hung in our house.

"We talked to several different museums about possibly taking the

trophy, but at the time, no one seemed to have much interest in it," Ray added. "Then, in 1970, Dr. Arnold wrote to us again. This time, he offered us $1,500 for the antlers. He promised us that he would take good care of the trophy and that he would see to it that it got the kind of recognition it deserved. We talked it over and decided to take his offer."

Dr. Arnold did indeed take good care of the buck…and avid whitetail hunters everywhere are glad of it.

A glimpse into whitetail history — John Breen stands over the incredible 202-point typical he shot back in 1918.
Photo courtesy the Breen family.

Chapter Seven

THE JOHN BUSH BUCK

181 1/8 TYPICAL, MINNESOTA, 1870

The Man And The Buck — Legends From The Past

BY ROB WEGNER

The year 1870 remains a fascinating year in the history of American deer hunting. Venison sold for five cents per pound and deerskins for 25 to 30 cents per pound. In 1870, in one city alone, St. Paul, Minnesota, exporters sold more that 3,859 whitetail hides.

During this time, the famous deer and deer hunting paintings of A.F. Tait (1819-1905) sold well. The great debate of the time revolved around still-hunting versus hounding, a controversial issue that drew more ink in the sportsmen's press that any other issue. Jack-lighting whitetails on wilderness lakes and streams was at its all-time height of popularity.

On November 9 of that year, John E. Bush (1828-1916), one of Ohio's most famous sportsmen and deer hunters, shot a 14-point whitetail along the Elk River in Benton County, Minnesota, with his 1849 Plainsman muzzleloader. Minnesota's deer season that year lasted for five months (September to January) and had no set bag limits. Minnesota's 25 cent deer hunting license was not required until 1897.

*The John Bush Buck as originally mounted
in 1870 by John Bush himself.
Photo by Larry Huffman.*

Main Characteristics: Shot in 1870, this buck was the Minnesota state record typical until John Breen shot his buck in 1918.

JOHN BUSH, MINNESOTA, 1870

	Right Antler	Left Antler	Difference
Main Beam Length	27 1/8	27 1/8	–
1st Point Length	7 4/8	7 7/8	3/8
2nd Point Length	11 2/8	11 1/8	1/8
3rd Point Length	11 6/8	11 2/8	4/8
4th Point Length	8 3/8	8 2/8	1/8
5th Point Length	1 1/8	–	1 1/8
1st Circumference	5 2/8	5 4/8	2/8
2nd Circumference	4 5/8	4 4/8	1/8
3rd Circumference	5 4/8	4 7/8	5/8
4th Circumference	4 7/8	4 5/8	2/8
Total	**87 3/8**	**85 1/8**	**3 4/8**

MISCELLANEOUS STATS

No. Of Points–Right	7
No. Of Points–Left	7
Total No. Of Points	14
Length Of Abnormals	9 5/8
Greatest Spread	23 6/8
Tip To Tip Spread	9 3/8
Inside Spread	21 6/8

FINAL TALLY

Inside Spread	21 6/8
Right Antler	87 3/8
Left Antler	85 1/8
Gross Score	194 2/8
Difference	-3 4/8
Subtotal	190 6/8
Abnormals	-9 5/8
NET TYPICAL SCORE	181 1/8

Bush's buck was destined to become (121 years later), the oldest originally mounted buck in the Boone and Crockett record book with an official typical score of 181 1/8. The buck holds a spot in the record book as the second oldest of 2,100 entries. Arthur Young shot the oldest Boone and Crockett buck back in 1830 in Pennsylvania. Only seven bucks from the 19th Century currently exist in the record book. The Jeff Benson Buck, shot in Texas in 1892 (286 non-typical), is perhaps the most famous of this particular group since it stood for years as the world record non-typical.

Bush mounted the head himself at a time when deer taxidermy was in its infancy. Given the mount's age, the deerskin was probably preserved with arsenic—a common method of preserving deerskins prior to the use of borax. After cleaning the skull, Bush attached it to a basic form constructed of wood and built the musculature out of paper and burlap.

Crude by today's standards, the mount has withstood 126 years. We can only guess how many hands it passed through before it landed in a garage sale where an Englewood man purchased it in 1991. He later sold it to Rick Busse, a local taxidermist living in Sidney, Ohio. It is now part of the Legendary Whitetail Collection owned by Larry Huffman.

Born in Monroe County, Pennsylvania, on September 30, 1828, Bush moved to Shelby County, Ohio, with his family in 1838. He shot his first deer at the age of 12 in 1840 near Swanders, Ohio, when he shot three deer in the same day. He went on to become one of the great sportsmen of his time, as A.B.C. Hitchcock, Bush's biographer, evidenced in a quote about him in a 1908 publication.

"Mr. Bush has killed over 200 deer, a moose, four bears, ducks and geese without number and does not have to draw on his imagination for deer stories. No other marksman of his age in this region has much show when he draws a bead on the target and the younger ones find in him a stubborn competitor."

During his long lifetime, this colorful character, affectionately called "Old Grizzley," crossed the continent to California nine times. On one of these California deer hunts, he shot fifty deer and one black bear, in addition to selling $777 worth of venison to sustain himself. While in California, this legendary marksman not only fought with Indians but with grizzly bears as well. When attacked one day by a grizzly, "Old Grizzley" hurriedly climbed a tree—but so did the bear! The bear caught Bush's leg—making four holes in his boot leg. Both fell to the ground. Luckily for Bush, the bear hurried off to join her cubs. According to Hitchcock, Bush cut off the boot leg with the "autograph of the bear" on it and placed it among his collection of hunting memorabilia.

As an expert taxidermist, his highly successful company was known as J.E. Bush Taxidermists & Sons. Bush maintained an elaborate interest in whitetail curiosities, relics and rare specimens. His home in Orange Township, one mile south of Sidney, soon became a wildlife and whitetail museum unequaled anywhere in America during this time. Historian Hitchcock visited Bush's house on one occasion and made these observations on what he saw:

"In the sitting room, a huge moose head, nine inches across the nose and

Rifles in hand, members of the Shelby County Deer Hunters Association pose with their deer in down-town Sidney, Ohio. White-bearded John Bush, the first president of the club, is shown second from the right. Photo courtesy Rick Busse.

with fan-like antlers, looked down from the wall. Mr. Bush and his son, Fred, killed the animal on the north shore of Lake Superior a few years ago. The animal was six feet and six inches high and weighed about 1,200 pounds; the horns have twenty-two points. To the left was a magnificent pair of elk horns of twelve points, five feet and seven inches high with four feet spread, a fine deer head and another of one killed in Minnesota.

"In the parlor is a stool with deer feet and elk horns for railing, a corner parlor chair which Mr. Bush fashioned from hickory and ash, a much prized photograph of eight deer suspended and killed in Maine with the hunters standing near, Joseph and Jess Laughlin, James Wilson, William Kingseed, Frank Brewer and Mr. Bush. Four of the deer he killed. There is also a photograph of two wild

turkeys and one of himself taken in California in 1853. Barbers being a scarce article there, his black hair covered his shoulders and a fringe of whiskers gave him the solemn look of a Dunkard preacher.

"From the parlor, we went upstairs to a large front room devoted entirely to specimens and relics which are there by the thousands, collected in different parts of the country...including thirteen deer heads on the walls, two of which got their horns locked while fighting and were found dead in South Dakota, three pair of buffalo horns and a host of other curiosities fairly bewildering in number."

In 1858, Bush and his deer hunting companions formed the Shelby County Deer Hunters Association, undoubtedly the oldest deer hunter's association in America. It is still in existence 138 years

The John Bush Buck

later. Bush became its first president and presided over its shooting contests, venison dinners and camaraderie get-togethers. He was eventually proclaimed the "President for Life."

Highlights of their meetings focused on telling deer hunting stories and sharing strategies to corner that old, elusive, mythic buck that Bush continually talked about, as well as competitive target shooting. One clear and painful rule governed these shooting events—the three poorest shots were requested to cut down a bee tree. According to Bush's biographer, "the blankets, knives, hatchets, etc., he won in these shooting contests at the deer hunters' picnics would give each of his eight children a good

Members of the Shelby County Deer Hunters Association drag a nice buck from the Maine woods around the turn of the century. The hunter on the left, identified only as "Buckskin," shot the deer. Photo courtesy Rick Busse.

setting out in articles of that line, and still have enough for himself and his wife."

One of Bush's close deer hunting friends, a blacksmith named Richard W. Valentine, kept a deer hunting diary for the years 1840 to 1879. The following excerpt from that diary vividly illustrates the dramatic effect that clear cutting and a lack of game laws had on Ohio's whitetail population: "October, 1877—Camped

on Middle Turkeyfoot Creek in Henry County, Ohio, about one mile down the creek from the railroad and only saw two deer. Deer are very scarce, hunting is about played out in Ohio."

As a result of Ohio's declining deer population by the 1870s, Bush and his boys (sometimes numbering as many as 50) got on trains called "The Hunters Specials," operated by the Canadian Pacific Line, and traveled to such places as Michigan, Wisconsin, Minnesota, Canada and Maine to pursue whitetails.

The members of the Shelby County Deer Hunters Association, whose ranks Theodore Roosevelt eventually joined, especially liked to hunt whitetails in Maine. These deer hunting excursions to Maine would frequently last for several months at a time, with the deer hunters traveling by rail cars, cutters, horses, sleighs, steamboats, stages and canoes. They slept in hollow trees, if necessary, but more often stayed at the Nineteenth Century Tavern, the social centerpiece of the deer-slayer tradition. This colorful place provided the hunters with bed and breakfast, while also serving as the local post office.

While on these deer hunts, Bush's advice was very simple: "No liver, no rum!" Bush shot at least one deer every year until shortly before his death in 1916. These delightful excursions would always end in down-town Sidney, where the deer were proudly

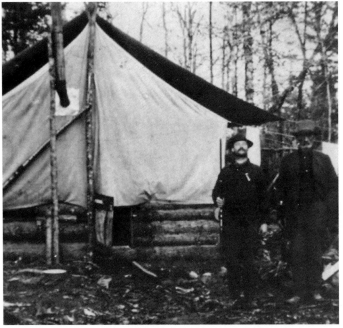

A tent with a stovepipe through it provided shelter for the members of the Shelby County Deer Hunters Association during their annual whitetail treks. Photo courtesy Rick Busse.

belched out its thunderous notes, Sam often found himself in hand-to-hand combat with wounded bucks. It seemed old Sam Edwards liked nothing better than a good-old vio-lent, physical brawl with a wounded buck.

One day while floating for deer near

displayed on the meat pole in front of The Elk Cafe with the deer hunters dressed in formal attire. Bush told the Association's members "that for every year you go deer hunting, you'll live five years longer." Bush understood his advice; he died at the age of 87.

Like most hunters, "Old Grizzley" loved to tell stories. His favorite deer hunting story dealt with the hair-splitting adventures of big Sam Edwards (1810-189?), another great Ohio deer hunter whose book, *The Ohio Hunter* (1866), Bush read and quoted with great delight. Like Bush, Sam Edwards tramped the deer forests of Ohio for miles on end each day, shot deer under the moon and slept wherever he found himself.

According to Bush, old Sam's diet was crude: "corn mush fried in grease, and full of worms at that." His equipment was primitive at best. After his crude rifle

Gerty's Island, Edwards and his brother came across two bucks quietly feeding on the green herbage in the water. Edwards recalls the event in his autobiography, a story that Bush fondly retold and embell-ished many times to members of the Shelby County Deer Hunters Association.

"My brother was steering, and I stood with my hand on my gun, ready to shoot as soon as the most favorable opportunity should present itself. They did not stir from their seemingly fixed position until we approached within a rod of them, then I shot one, and applied with double energy the oars until we reached the spot where the buck fell.

"Just as we neared it, he sprung to his feet and started for the shore. As he was passing the boat, I sprung upon his back and clinched him by the horns. The water was not quite so favorable a place for fighting with a sturdy buck as terra firma and the brave animal soon had the best of the bargain, getting me underneath his feet and giving me such a drubbing as I never got from man or beast before or since.

"However, I did not let go my hold about the horns, and in process of time found myself again in the ascendancy, and then treated the offender to an immersion in the waves in return for the civil compliment that he had paid me. I held his head under until he drowned.

"My brother now came up with the boat and took us both in, after the engagement was ended, quite to my relief, having myself submit-ted to rather a longer immersion in cold water than is prescribed by the most approved system of hydropathy."

Whether Bush actually hunted with such famous Ohio deerslayers as Sam Edwards and Oliver Hazard Perry (1817-1864), we can only surmise. We do know that Bush frequently accompanied Buffalo Bill Cody's "Wild West Show" as it traveled throughout the area.

Bush's basic philosophy in life, according to A.B.C. Hitchcock, "was to enjoy the passing moment and not depend too much on an uncertain future, subscribing without mental reservation to the saying that one bird in the hand is worth two in the Bush."

Another successful hunting trip for the Shelby County Deer Hunters Association ends with the harvest on display in Sidney. With deer no longer present in huntable numbers in Ohio, these tough, determined sportsmen made arduous trips out of state to pursue their sport. Photo courtesy Rick Busse.

Chapter Eight

THE GEORGE CHALUS BUCK

191 6/8 TYPICAL, SASKATCHEWAN, 1973

Oh, For A Good Wife To Push The Bush

BY GREG MILLER

One look at the George Chalus Buck is enough to convince anyone this deer does indeed qualify as a "legendary whitetail." With lengthy main beams of 27 and 26 inches, an inside spread of nearly 20 inches, extremely long tines and better than average mass, the Chalus Buck truly is a classic giant typical.

George shot his big buck near Hudson Bay, Saskatchewan, during the 1973 deer season. Back in those days, George owned and operated a machine shop in the town of Hudson Bay. He also offered a mobile welding service. In truth, it was a request for his mobile welding services that eventually led him to take the giant buck.

As George tells it, "Late one evening in mid November, I received a phone call from the boss at a logging camp. He told me he needed some welding work done on a piece of equipment. Normally, I would have sent my hired man out to do the job, but for some reason, he didn't show up for work the next morning, so I had to make the trip. I took off from Hudson Bay at first light. Since deer season was open and I'd be driving through some good deer country, I decided to take my rifle with me."

The area George would be driving through contained a mixture of alfalfa and wheat fields bordered by large chunks of heavy cover. As he cruised toward his desti-

Photo by Ron Brown

Main Characteristics: Classic typical appearance. No abnormal points.

George Chalus, Saskatchewan, 1973

	Right Antler	Left Antler	Difference
Main Beam Length	27 0/8	26 0/8	1 0/8
1st Point Length	8 0/8	8 0/8	–
2nd Point Length	11 6/8	12 1/8	3/8
3rd Point Length	12 1/8	12 5/8	4/8
4th Point Length	10 1/8	10 5/8	4/8
5th Point Length	–	5 0/8	5 0/8
1st Circumference	4 5/8	4 6/8	1/8
2nd Circumference	4 3/8	5 0/8	5/8
3rd Circumference	4 4/8	4 4/8	–
4th Circumference	4 6/8	4 4/8	2/8
Total	**87 2/8**	**93 1/8**	**8 3/8**

Miscellaneous Stats	
No. Of Points–Right	5
No. Of Points–Left	6
Total No. Of Points	11
Length Of Abnormals	–
Greatest Spread	21 7/8
Tip To Tip Spread	12 3/8
Inside Spread	19 6/8

Final Tally	
Inside Spread	19 6/8
Right Antler	87 2/8
Left Antler	93 1/8
Gross Score	200 1/8
Difference	-8 3/8
Subtotal	191 6/8
Abnormals	—
Net Typical Score	191 6/8

nation, he kept an eye out for any deer that might be feeding in the fields. Six inches of fresh snow provided a good background for spotting deer.

"About 14 miles from Hudson Bay, I saw my first deer," George remembered. "He was standing in a snow-covered alfalfa field roughly 400 yards from the road. I stopped the truck, grabbed my rifle and walked off the road a ways. I turned my variable-power scope up to full power and centered the deer in the scope. What I saw nearly took my breath away. It was a buck with a set of antlers larger than anything I'd ever seen!"

George looked at the giant deer for a few minutes, trying to decide what to do, then walked back to his truck. Although it was a tough thing to do, he drove off and left the monster buck standing in the alfalfa.

"I decided against taking a shot at him," he stated. "It was legal shooting time, but there wasn't a lot of light yet. And, I wasn't comfortable shooting at 400 yards with my .308. Also, they were expecting me at the logging camp. I just couldn't spend any more time trying to get closer to the buck."

Upon arrival at the logging camp, George immediately went to work but the sight of the big buck kept nagging at his thoughts.

"While I worked, I thought about where that buck might go to bed down for the day," George said. "I figured he had a couple options. He could either cross the road and go into a large chunk of bush, or he could stay where he was and bed in a much smaller piece of cover that bordered the alfalfa field. I decided that, if I got done working early enough, I was going back to where I'd seen the buck and do some walking around. Maybe I'd be able to track him and find where he was hiding out."

George finished his welding job shortly after noon. By 1:00 p.m., he was back where he'd seen the buck.

"I walked the road and checked all the tracks crossing over into the large chunk of bush. None of them were big enough to be the buck's," he stated. "Then, I walked across the alfalfa field to where the buck had been standing earlier and looked around. Judging from the tracks, I knew he had to be bedded in that small piece of cover next to the field.

"I immediately walked back to my truck and headed for home. There, I got my wife and a friend by the name of Ed Tchorzewski. I told them about the buck and asked if they would walk through that piece of bush and try to push the buck out to me. I think they could see the excitement in my face, so it didn't take much talking to convince them to go back with me."

After arriving back at the scene,

George diagramed his plan of attack.

"Ed and my wife went to the far end of the thicket to start the push," he stated. "I took up a position at the other end of the cover. If the buck came out by me, he'd have to run across about 50 yards of open ground. I figured that would give me plenty of time to get off a good shot."

It didn't take long for the two drivers to reach the middle of the thicket. But as of yet, George hadn't seen or heard a deer.

"I was getting kind of worried," he admitted. "And, I became even more worried when Ed and my wife got within 50 yards of me. I figured the buck must have either laid tight or slipped out the back of the drive. But just when I thought the drive was over, a huge buck burst from the thick cover 100 yards away. He caught me by surprise, and I shot too quick the first time and missed him clean. But, I settled down and took my time on the second shot. He went down for good then."

Although he knew the buck was exceptional, George didn't really know how exceptional. Luckily, a close friend saw the antlers and urged George to have them scored for Boone and Crockett.

"I took the rack to the Fish and Wildlife office in Hudson Bay and a fellow measured it," George said. "A few weeks later, I received an invitation to attend the province's annual big game banquet to be held in Estevan. I was told the rack would be officially scored then."

At the banquet, official measurers came up with a final typical score of 191 6/8 for George's buck. This score was good enough to garner George first place for the largest typical recorded in the province for 1973.

Chapter Nine

DESI

---

296 NON-TYPICAL, OHIO, 1983

Case Study Of A World-Class Non-typical

BY DUNCAN DOBIE

For most deer hunters, finding even a single shed antler is an uncommon event. To locate a matched set from a mature buck is even more rare, and to pick up antlers from the same trophy whitetail two or three years in a row requires extraordinary effort and luck.

So, imagine how seldom a hunter gets to study firsthand a buck's complete history of shed antlers, from his first rack on past what is normally considered the animal's "prime." The accompanying photos show just such a collection of antlers, produced by a buck raised in captivity for 12 years.

This enormous buck, named Desi, was acquired as a fawn by Bob Baird of Canfield, Ohio, from a nearby pet farm in 1973. The young buck then was raised in a stall of a barn on Bob's property. For almost all of his life, the buck stayed in a stall that had only one window to provide any sunlight. Eventually, though, a fenced "run" was constructed adjacent to the stall so Desi could go outside whenever he wished.

The Bairds collected each set of shed antlers from the buck. He was never able to

Desi at age 10 1/2 with a score of 296.
Photo by Larry Huffman.

DESI, OHIO, 1983

	Right Antler	Left Antler	Difference
Main Beam Length	23 4/8	21 3/8	2 1/8
1st Point Length	6 0/8	8 1/8	2 1/8
2nd Point Length	10 6/8	10 0/8	6/8
3rd Point Length	7 0/8	6 4/8	4/8
4th Point Length	–	–	–
5th Point Length	–	–	–
1st Circumference	6 4/8	6 3/8	1/8
2nd Circumference	5 5/8	5 2/8	3/8
3rd Circumference	5 5/8	4 6/8	7/8
4th Circumference	4 5/8	3 1/8	1 4/8
Total	**69 5/8**	**65 4/8**	**8 3/8**

Main Characteristics: Desi's 4x4 frame has a net typical score of only 143. His 39 abnormal points add 153 more points to the score.

MISCELLANEOUS STATS		FINAL TALLY	
No. Of Points–Right	28	**Inside Spread**	16 2/8
No. Of Points–Left	19	**Right Antler**	69 5/8
Total No. Of Points	47	**Left Antler**	65 4/8
Length Of Abnormals	153 0/8	**Gross Score**	151 3/8
Greatest Spread	27 5/8	**Difference**	-8 3/8
Tip To Tip Spread	10 0/8	**Subtotal**	143 0/8
Inside Spread	16 2/8	**Abnormals**	+153 0/8
		NET NON-TYPICAL SCORE	**296 0/8**

rub his rack normally, and much of the dried velvet was peeled off by hand after the antlers were shed. As a result, several sets appear to be unusually smooth. According to Bob, Desi always was fed a normal diet of sweet feed and corn, never any supplements or hormones to boost antler growth.

For the first 6 1/2 years of this deer's life, his antlers appeared normal in every way, steadily increasing in size and mass. But after that, the racks began to grow more erratically. Then, in the fall of 1983, when the deer was 10 1/2 years old, his antlers suddenly experienced an extraordinary surge of growth, sprouting many abnormal points on each beam. That was the buck's largest set of antlers.

Desi certainly lived long enough to achieve maximum antler growth, and from a nutritional standpoint, he never had to experience the rigors of life in the wild. Plus, his consistent food supply probably afforded him a much higher

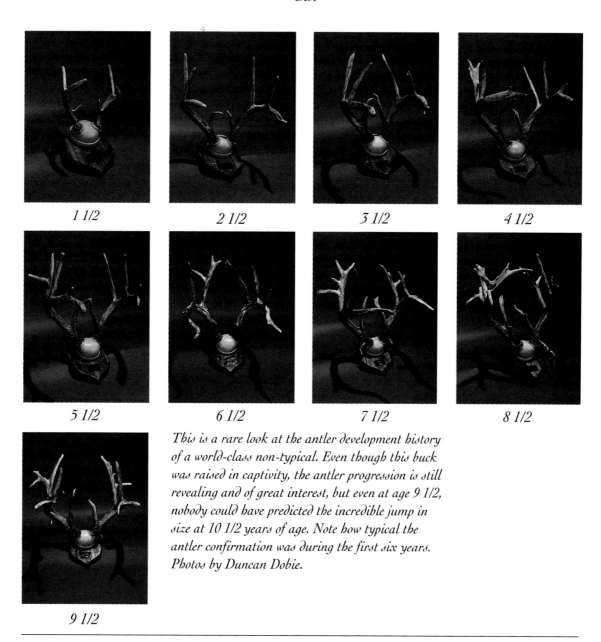

1 1/2 *2 1/2* *3 1/2* *4 1/2*

5 1/2 *6 1/2* *7 1/2* *8 1/2*

This is a rare look at the antler development history of a world-class non-typical. Even though this buck was raised in captivity, the antler progression is still revealing and of great interest, but even at age 9 1/2, nobody could have predicted the incredible jump in size at 10 1/2 years of age. Note how typical the antler confirmation was during the first six years. Photos by Duncan Dobie.

9 1/2

percentage of protein than most bucks in the wild receive. And, of course, Ohio is known to have the genetics for outstanding antlers and body size.

But one other factor also might have contributed to Desi's huge headgear. Research has proved that a buck's antler growth is triggered by hormone changes within his body—changes which in turn are triggered by increasing or decreasing amounts of daylight during the four sea-

sons of the year. Because Desi spent most of his life confined inside a stall in a barn, the imbalance in normal sunlight intake very possibly could have triggered some type of hormonal imbalance, thereby resulting in gross antler distortion.

Whatever the exact reason(s) for Desi's amazing racks, one thing is certain: He was a fascinating case study that gave us a unique glimpse at the world of deer antlers.

Chapter Ten

THE ROSS ENGLOT BUCK

219 1/8 NON-TYPICAL, SASKATCHEWAN, 1982

A Whopper Case Of Beginner's Luck

BY GREG MILLER

One thing has become apparent to me over the many years I've been involved with trophy whitetails: A great number of the largest bucks taken each year aren't harvested by experienced hunters. In fact, I'd be willing to make a wager that the vast majority of the all-time greatest whitetails were shot by beginner or novice hunters. Once again, such is the case in this story.

The hunter involved in this particular tale of beginner's luck is Ross Englot. At the time, back in 1982, Ross was 14 years old and living with his family near the small town of Hanley, Saskatchewan, located approximately 30 miles south of Saskatoon.

The Englot family was and still is actively involved in farming. And like most farmers, they spend a lot of time watching over their crops. According to Ross's father, Chester Englot, this also enables the family to keep a pretty close eye on the local deer herd.

"We see a lot of big bucks feeding in our fields throughout the summer and fall months," he told me. "By the time hunting season opens, we've got a pretty good idea

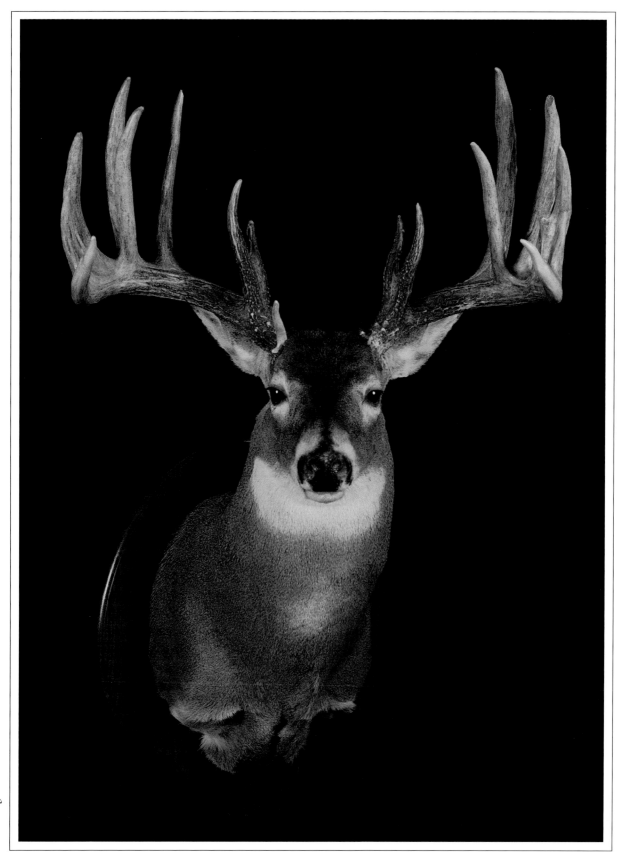

Photo by Ron Brown

ROSS ENGLOT, SASKATCHEWAN, 1982

	Right Antler	Left Antler	Difference
Main Beam Length	25 0/8	24 2/8	6/8
1st Point Length	7 2/8	6 1/8	1 1/8
2nd Point Length	10 7/8	13 0/8	2 1/8
3rd Point Length	10 3/8	10 2/8	1/8
4th Point Length	7 7/8	7 4/8	3/8
5th Point Length	5 1/8	3 6/8	1 3/8
1st Circumference	5 0/8	5 0/8	–
2nd Circumference	4 7/8	4 7/8	–
3rd Circumference	5 5/8	5 6/8	1/8
4th Circumference	5 7/8	5 0/8	7/8
Total	**87 7/8**	**85 4/8**	**6 7/8**

Main Characteristics: Wide inside spread of 23 1/8". Split brow tines on both sides.

MISCELLANEOUS STATS	
No. Of Points–Right	9
No. Of Points–Left	9
Total No. Of Points	18
Length Of Abnormals	29 4/8
Greatest Spread	26 0/8
Tip To Tip Spread	20 2/8
Inside Spread	23 1/8

FINAL TALLY	
Inside Spread	23 1/8
Right Antler	87 7/8
Left Antler	85 4/8
Gross Score	196 4/8
Difference	-6 7/8
Subtotal	189 5/8
Abnormals	+29 4/8
NET NON-TYPICAL SCORE	**219 1/8**

which pieces of bush are holding the biggest bucks."

This particular part of Saskatchewan is not made up of the flat, prairie-type terrain one often associates with this province. Instead, the terrain here is comprised of rolling hills and deep draws. While a great deal of the acreage is open cropland, some of the surrounding pieces of "bush" are rather expansive, creating ideal whitetail habitat.

Ross had first hunted during the 1981 season but hadn't managed to connect. This year, however, Chester had decided to put forth a lot more effort to help his son tag his first buck. As luck would have it, Chester was able to down a big buck himself on opening day. Now, he'd be able to dedicate the rest of the season to helping Ross get within range of a buck.

The father and son hunted hard over the next few days. Although they saw several good bucks, the deer always managed to give them the slip.

"Our favorite form of hunting is to take a few guys and then make small pushes through selected pieces of cover," Chester told me. "Normally, we have good success doing this. But, it seemed no matter what I did that year, I just couldn't get Ross in the right spot."

Still, the two didn't give up hope, and when Chester and Ross awoke on the fifth day of the season, they found that a couple inches of fresh snow had fallen.

"I got a good feeling right away when I saw that snow," Chester remembers. "So as soon as it was light enough to see, Ross and I headed out in my pickup and drove around the edge to some of our fields. It didn't take long to see that the new snow had made the deer real active. There were fresh tracks everywhere!

"I soon found a set of tracks in a field that I knew had to be from a huge buck," he said. "The buck had been all over the field and then had headed into a nearby patch of thick cover. I drove around the patch of cover but couldn't find his tracks coming out. I knew he had to be hiding out in there."

Chester quickly drove to the far end of the cover and dropped off his son.

"I told Ross to get behind a fence post, then I headed back to the other end of the thicket and started making a push toward him. Well, I'd taken only a few steps into the bush when I heard a deer take off. I hollered for Ross to get ready, then I ran out into the field to watch what happened."

Ross could hear the buck running his way but couldn't see him. Then, suddenly, a buck with a huge rack burst from the thick cover directly in front of him.

Initially, it appeared as though the giant deer was on a collision course with the young hunter.

"Obviously, the buck didn't see Ross hiding behind the fence post. He continued running right at him until he was about 20 feet away. At that point, Ross moved just a bit. The buck spotted him and jumped sideways just as he shot," Chester stated.

The buck staggered but quickly regained his balance and continued on his course. Before the young hunter could get lined up for a second shot with his .308, the big deer disappeared into another thicket. Chester, watching the whole event from his vantage point, had doubts about the severity of the hit. His concerns were soon alleviated.

"We found the buck laying down just 100 yards into the next patch of cover, and Ross was able to sneak up and finish him," he said.

"I knew right away we had something special, so we loaded the buck into my truck and headed for Hanley. A fellow by the name of Darryl Libke worked in the Fish & Wildlife office there, and he knew how to score antlers. He took one look at the rack and told me the buck would score quite high as a non-typical."

Indeed it did! The giant rack possesses a greatest spread of 26 inches, while the inside spread measures 23 1/8 inches. There are 18 scorable points on the rack, nine on each side. Libke's initial score came in at 213 2/8 points. Some years later, the rack was officially rescored and awarded a higher score of 219 1/8 non-typical.

Not a bad deer for a beginning hunter—or any hunter for that matter!

Chapter Eleven

THE FLEMMING SHEDS

207 2/8 Typical, Saskatchewan, 1983

The Possible World Record That Was—And Lived!

By Dick Idol

Back in the early 1980s, many of the whitetail hardcores who followed scores, myself included, were convinced that a new world record typical could well be walking around in the wild during any given year. James Jordan's 206 1/8-point world record, killed in 1914, had withstood every challenge for decades, but several others had come close, such as Larry Gibson's Missouri buck at 205, Mel Johnson's world record archery typical at 204 4/8, etc.

Even though none had quite overtaken the Jordan Buck, several known typical bucks had grown enough gross inches of antler to be the world record, and some even had net scores that exceeded 206 1/8 before deductions for abnormal points. But, there always was some big "if," usually abnormal points, that kept the buck's final net score below the magic threshold. After all, it's the "clean" giant typical that's the real rarity, much more so than non-typicals or big typicals with abnormal points. So, we began contemplating that perhaps a giant typical that was clean enough to net better than the extraordinarily clean Jordan Buck, which had no abnormal point deductions, might be such a rarity that it could take decades for one to show up...or,

Main Characteristics: Shed antlers from Saskatchewan. Very long tines. G-2 on right side measures 17 2/8" in length.

FLEMMING SHEDS, SASKATCHEWAN, 1983

	Right Antler	Left Antler	Difference
Main Beam Length	27 6/8	27 5/8	1/8
1st Point Length	7 5/8	8 0/8	3/8
2nd Point Length	17 2/8	15 6/8	1 4/8
3rd Point Length	14 3/8	13 4/8	7/8
4th Point Length	8 2/8	9 1/8	7/8
5th Point Length	–	–	–
1st Circumference	5 5/8	5 5/8	–
2nd Circumference	5 1/8	5 1/8	–
3rd Circumference	5 5/8	5 5/8	–
4th Circumference	5 2/8	5 3/8	1/8
Total	**96 6/8**	**95 5/8**	**3 7/8**

MISCELLANEOUS STATS	
No. Of Points–Right	7
No. Of Points–Left	6
Total No. Of Points	13
Length Of Abnormals	4 6/8
Greatest Spread	26 0/8
Tip To Tip Spread	15 4/8
Inside Spread	23 4/8

FINAL TALLY	
Inside Spread	23 4/8
Right Antler	96 6/8
Left Antler	95 5/8
Gross Score	215 7/8
Difference	-3 7/8
Subtotal	212 0/8
Abnormals	-4 6/8
NET TYPICAL SCORE	207 2/8

on the other hand, one could come along tomorrow that put the antler growth in the right places.

Then, in 1983, new hope emerged when the first hard evidence came to light that a potential new world record typical might, in fact, be out there. That hope was kindled upon the discovery of a huge set of sheds from Saskatchewan known as the "Flemming Sheds."

Stephen McClung, an antler buyer from Texas, got wind of a rumor while in a bar in Saskatchewan that a giant shed antler had been found on a nearby farm. He promptly went to the farmer and found out that what he had heard was far more than rumor. The farmer had in his possession a single, five-point antler that was simply huge. McClung asked if he could look for the other side. The farmer gave the go-ahead and then told him precisely where he'd found the antler. Within a matter of hours, he and his wife had found the opposite side—a near mirror image of the side found earlier.

When these sheds were put together

in a manner approximating their position on the deer's head, the final net score was 207 2/8 typical points. To my knowledge, this was the first undisputable physical evidence to ever show up of a buck exceeding the Jordan head. There were single shed antlers with potentially higher scores, but without the matching antler, the final score could only be speculated upon. As you would expect, the discovery of this buck caused quite a stir among the whitetail fraternity.

The sheds were found in April of 1983 near Flemming, Saskatchewan, which is located in the southeastern part of the providence along the Pipestone Valley. The Pipestone Valley has a long and illustrious history of producing huge whitetails, so the fact that the sheds were found there is no great surprise. Geographically, the terrain alongside the valley consists of rolling prairie and farmland. The valley itself is quite deep and choked with heavy cover. Between the top and bottom of the valley are many ravines, benches, knobs, etc. The Pipestone Valley is ideal whitetail habitat and is rather difficult to hunt. It is also

The right-side look at a world record buck that lived out his life unscathed by a hunter's bullet. Photo by Dick Idol.

The left profile of one of the biggest typicals of all time. Photo by Dick Idol.

located in an area closed to hunting for non-Canadians.

Even the 207 2/8 score doesn't properly portray the impressiveness of this buck. For starters, he's a basic 5x5, which means his main frame must be bigger than that of a 6x6 or 7x7 of the same score. His gross typical score of 215 7/8 more accurately reflects his giant frame size. With an estimated inside spread of 23 4/8 inches (26 inches outside) and G-2s of 17 2/8 and 15 6/8 inches, one can get a better grasp of his true size. His net typical score before deducting 4 6/8 inches for his three abnormal points is an awesome 212!

As far as we know, this buck was seldom seen and never killed. I've been collecting big shed antlers for years, and I have several world-class sheds (pairs and singles) in my collection. I would estimate that of all the giant sheds from bucks I've known about over the years, no more than 10 percent of them were ever killed. It merely points out the difficulty of killing the real giants and says a lot about their survival capabilities.

Chapter Twelve

THE LLOYD GOAD BUCK

197 6/8 TYPICAL, IOWA, 1962

The Former World Record Archery Typical

BY DUNCAN DOBIE

Killing a record buck with a bow and arrow is no easy matter, even with the help of today's state-of-the-art archery equipment. But if you turn the calendar back several decades to a time when bowhunting was still in its infancy and you accomplish that feat with a 45-pound recurve and wooden arrows, it becomes even more remarkable. Such was the situation in 1962 when 34-year-old service station operator Lloyd Goad arrowed a 197 6/8 typical in Monroe County, Iowa.

After killing his record buck, Lloyd was asked to write accounts of the hunt for various publications. One story appeared in the May 1967 issue of *Archery World*. Several shorter versions also appeared in various editions of the Pope and Young record book. The following story is taken from Lloyd's own accounts of his historical hunt.

"Around 1953, the Iowa Conservation Commission opened a special deer season

Photo by Larry Huffman

Main Characteristics:
Magnificent 7x7 Iowa
bow kill.

LLOYD GOAD, IOWA, 1962

	Right Antler	Left Antler	Difference
Main Beam Length	25 6/8	26 4/8	6/8
1st Point Length	5 0/8	3 3/8	1 5/8
2nd Point Length	6 3/8	9 0/8	2 5/8
3rd Point Length	11 2/8	10 0/8	1 2/8
4th Point Length	11 0/8	11 3/8	3/8
5th Point Length	9 6/8	10 1/8	3/8
6th Point Length	2 4/8	5 5/8	3 1/8
1st Circumference	5 1/8	5 2/8	1/8
2nd Circumference	4 7/8	5 0/8	1/8
3rd Circumference	5 4/8	5 5/8	1/8
4th Circumference	5 2/8	7 5/8	2 3/8
Total	**92 3/8**	**99 4/8**	**12 7/8**

MISCELLANEOUS STATS

No. Of Points–Right	7
No. Of Points–Left	7
Total No. Of Points	14
Length Of Abnormals	–
Greatest Spread	21 2/8
Tip To Tip Spread	13 6/8
Inside Spread	18 6/8

FINAL TALLY

Inside Spread	18 6/8
Right Antler	92 3/8
Left Antler	99 4/8
Gross Score	210 5/8
Difference	-12 7/8
Subtotal	197 6/8
Abnormals	—
NET TYPICAL SCORE	197 6/8

with a limited number of permits for a two-day, shotgun-only hunt. Hunting deer was a new experience, but my earlier success in squirrel hunting helped me immensely. It wasn't long before Don (Lloyd's brother-in-law) and I found out where the deer liked to stay and which trails they favored. We didn't always fill out tags, but for six or seven years, we had some very rewarding hunts.

"Gradually, the enthusiasm for deer hunting in Iowa spread. More and more hunters began to 'invade' our territory. It became a real rat race. Then, I began to take notice of some of the successes that local bowhunters were experiencing. One of the two original bowhunters in our area brought in the biggest buck I'd ever seen! Right then, I decided that the challenge of bowhunting would bring back the part of hunting that I had seemingly lost.

"Midway through the 50-day 1961 bow season, I bought a 45-pound York Crescent recurve bow and some cedar shafts tipped with Hill's Hornet broadheads. After several days of practicing, I started shooting some reasonable arrow groupings. I thought I could get my deer if I had a chance to pick my shot."

Taken in the wash bay of a Champlin (Iowa) gas station in 1962, an obviously proud Lloyd Goad shows off his then archery world record 14-pointer. Photo courtesy the Goad family.

With less than two weeks left in the season, Lloyd headed for the woods. Hunting on the ground, as he had always done with a shotgun, he was offered a shot almost immediately.

"I had a button buck come within six feet of me," Lloyd wrote. "I shot about four inches over his shoulder! The second shot came a few days later when a dandy little forkhorn walked by broadside at 20 yards. My arrow hit an oak limb right in front of him, went straight up and landed about 20 feet behind the deer!"

That was the last action Lloyd saw during the 1961 season, but he was hopelessly hooked on bowhunting. The early weeks of the 1962 season brought two more disappointing misses. But, little could Lloyd know that his next shot would bring down one of the greatest typicals in history.

"When the last day of archery season appeared on the calendar—December 2, 1962—I was still without a deer," Lloyd wrote. "I took the day off and started on the 18-mile ride to my stand with the windows and vents open on my pickup to help rid my clothes of household odors. Before heading into the woods, I applied a liberal dose of buck lure on the sleeves and legs of my camouflage suit and a bit extra on my cap for good measure.

"Since most bowhunters hunted on the ground in those days, my preferred method of hunting was to set up near a major trail not far from a crossing on a road with very little traffic. You could get there quickly and quietly without spreading a lot of scent, and I found that deer liked to use these trails.

"When I reached where I intended to hunt, I met a hunting buddy, Bob DeMoss, who planned to squirrel hunt in the same general area. I also ran into two other bowhunters. One had shot a doe the evening before and was back to look for it just north of where I wanted to hunt. His friend said he would cover a trail to the west. Bob decided to hunt squirrels just south of me across a dirt road. So, I decided to hunt a well-used trail not far from the road, pretty much in the middle of all this activity, in hopes that something might happen."

Lloyd slipped into a small patch of woods near the intersection of two dirt roads. He took a stand next to a large elm tree not far from a brushy fence row. The area was cloaked in a heavy mist, the kind big bucks love to sneak around in. Lloyd had just settled in when he heard a noise on the trail.

"I peeked around the elm tree and there he came, slipping through the wild plums and sumac bushes with his head down," Lloyd wrote. "He had so many

> *"I peeked around the elm tree and there he came, slipping through the wild plums and sumac bushes with his head down," Lloyd wrote. "He had so many points I couldn't distinguish his antlers from the limbs. My heart started pounding so hard that I thought he must be deaf not to hear it."*

points I couldn't distinguish his antlers from the limbs. My heart started pounding so hard that I thought he must be deaf not to hear it. He walked up to the fence and stopped behind some brush not 20 feet away. I waited.

"Finally, he just sort of melted over the fence with no effort. My bow was already in position, and all I had to do was pull it back. When I did, he stopped and looked straight at me, 18 steps away. He was already beginning to whirl as I released the arrow. It looked like my arrow caught him in the fore-part of the right hind leg or possibly through the lower part of his gut. I stayed put and listened. He ran a short distance. Then, it sounded like he stopped in some thick brush several yards to my left. I was in real agony. I felt like the arrow had either inflicted a minor flesh wound or hit him in the gut."

Lloyd waited half an hour then made his way back to the truck, where he met Bob. Wisely, they decided to give the buck time and to go to town for help in the search. Fearing a long, drawn-out search, Lloyd returned four hours later with several friends.

The search, however, was a short one. Lloyd's buck lay 150 yards from where it had been shot. The broadhead had severed a leg artery, causing the buck to bleed to death in minutes.

The Goad Buck, which field-dressed 224 pounds, sported a massive, symmetrical 7x7 rack. At 197 6/8 P&Y points, it became a new archery typical world record. That record was broken in 1965 when Mel Johnson shot an Illinois typical scoring 204 4/8, putting Lloyd's buck in the No. 2 spot. In 1986, Curt Van Lith arrowed a massive 11-point buck in Minnesota that tied Lloyd's buck, and the two bucks have shared the No. 2 spot ever since.

Lloyd, who died December 18, 1993, at the age of 65, continued bowhunting for many sea-sons after downing his Iowa record. He was often asked how it felt to have to settle for smaller bucks since the chances of ever encountering another buck like his 14-pointer were slim at best.

"Every deer is a new experience," Lloyd always answered. "And, every shot is a challenge. Not every deer will make the top of the record book, but they all make my book—bowhunting pleasure!"

> *"The Goad Buck, which field-dressed 224 pounds, sported a massive, symmetrical 7x7 rack. At 197 6/8 P&Y points, it became a new archery typical world record."*

Chapter Thirteen

THE JERRY HAMPTON BUCK

226 4/8 NON-TYPICAL, KANSAS, 1988

*Wide, Heavy & Tall —
This Buck Has It All*

BY LES DAVENPORT

Thirty years of whitetail hunting taught Jerry Hampton of LaCygne, Kansas, three crucial components for success in the sport—patience, persistence and preciseness. Patience and persistence during periods of poor deer movement eventually earned favorable encounters. Preciseness of shot placement endorsed respect for the species and ultimately rewarded patience and persistence. Given Jerry's mastery of these three hunting principles, his pinnacle payday may well have been deserved fate.

The Sunflower State firearm season falls between the peak rut and the relatively minor secondary rut, which can deal Kansas trophy hunters a fit if the weather fails to cooperate. And in early December 1988, temperate weather, perhaps the worst of all conditions for post-rut bucks, prompted dormancy in mature bucks and posed a dilemma for Jerry and his father, Olen. Few prior sightings and only three days left to hunt stirred visions of coming up empty-handed. Neither father or son, however, verbalized pessimism. Companionship meant more to them than just taking a deer. If

*Main Characteristics:
Very impressive brow
tines. Heavy bases of
6 7/8" and 6 6/8".*

Jerry Hampton, Kansas, 1988

	Right Antler	Left Antler	Difference
Main Beam Length	26 3/8	24 6/8	1 5/8
1st Point Length	10 0/8	9 7/8	1/8
2nd Point Length	13 2/8	12 0/8	1 2/8
3rd Point Length	12 4/8	12 3/8	1/8
4th Point Length	7 6/8	9 0/8	1 2/8
5th Point Length	–	–	–
1st Circumference	6 7/8	6 6/8	1/8
2nd Circumference	6 1/8	5 4/8	5/8
3rd Circumference	5 4/8	5 3/8	1/8
4th Circumference	5 4/8	4 6/8	6/8
Total	**93 7/8**	**90 3/8**	**6 0/8**

Miscellaneous Stats		Final Tally	
No. Of Points–Right	12	**Inside Spread**	21 6/8
No. Of Points–Left	10	**Right Antler**	93 7/8
Total No. Of Points	22	**Left Antler**	90 3/8
Length Of Abnormals	26 4/8	**Gross Score**	**206 0/8**
Greatest Spread	24 6/8	**Difference**	-6 0/8
Tip To Tip Spread	15 6/8	**Subtotal**	**200 0/8**
Inside Spread	21 6/8	**Abnormals**	+26 4/8
		Net Non-Typical Score	**226 4/8**

forbearance to stay the course did not pay off, so be it. They would be there to the end.

Olen suggested a change in game plan for the last three attempts. Jerry concurred. They'd move to a different area, Area 11 tract in Linn county. The 400-acre farm they had access to there offered a mixture of wooded hill country and bottom ground. Harvested corn, bean and milo fields adjoined by forest edge afforded whitetails ideal habitat.

Plus, a huge buck had been reported in the area. Perhaps this deer would slip up and make an appearance during daylight.

A fence line dozed through a section of woods on the property offered an apex ambush site. Olen used a ground blind, and Jerry perched in a tree stand aloft a thornless locust. Any deer that passed through a 300-yard stretch of the cleared lane was in striking range of Jerry's Remington.

Day one at the new tract was disappointingly uneventful. Day two, however, wasn't. Jerry and Olen situated themselves before daybreak and hoped for better deer movement than the previous day had brought. Olen had relocated farther up the cutline in an attempt to watch a different trail. Soon, the sun peeked above the tree line and cast its warming rays on cool morning air. Another bluebird day was in the making. Not good for post-rut deer movement, speculated Jerry.

The duo sat motionless for three hours. Only birds and squirrels disrupted the woodland stillness. Then, just after 9 a.m., a buck materialized at the exact spot Olen had been stationed the day prior. The big deer headed in Jerry's direction. This was no average whitetail, thought Jerry.

At 100 yards, the buck presented a broadside shot. Jerry breathed deep, took aim and squeezed the trigger of his .270 Rem. BDL. The deer bolted as if unscathed and quickly vanished in thick timber.

Jerry was confident he had not missed the mark. Hoping for the best, he descended the tree and cautiously entered the woods. A heart shot had dropped the awesome whitetail 75 yards

Jerry Hampton shows us what a world-class buck looks like "in person." Photo courtesy Jerry Hampton.

from the cutline, 10 feet from the edge of a cavernous ravine.

Jerry could hardly believe the size of the awesome rack. The 5x5 frame carried three kicker points, one drop tine and eight sticker points. Its mass was incredible, especially the bases, which were later measured at 6 7/8 and 6 6/8-inches in circumference. Wide, tall and heavy—this buck had it all!

Thin from rutting activity, the 6 1/2-year-old buck was eventually weighed at 178 pounds field dressed. His official score came in at 226 4/8 non-typical. As far as anyone knows, this deer had only been seen previously by a local woman when it crossed her front yard. Chances are that Jerry's face-off with the great Kansas buck occurred during a rare daylight appearance.

Jerry reports that the genetics of his non-typical are alive and well in Linn County. Over the past few years, another whitetail with grandeur rack dimensions has been spotted several times on the perimeter of the same woods. Though Jerry does not expect lightning to strike twice in the same spot, be assured that his patience, persistence and preciseness of aim will be on-stand in Linn county for many years to come.

Chapter Fourteen

THE HOLE-IN-THE-HORN BUCK

---

328 2/8 NON-TYPICAL, OHIO, 1940

The Greatest Whitetail Of All Time?

BY DICK IDOL

I t could be argued that Ohio's so-called "Hole-In-The-Horn Buck" is the most famous whitetail in the world. In fact, this legendary deer, with his incredible rack and story to match, might well be the most famous big game animal ever to come from the North American continent!

My own involvement in this story began sometime around 1977 when I was in the business of outfitting guided hunts, primarily for trophy whitetails. As a group of hunters and I sat around a campfire one evening, one of the clients pulled out photos of two of the largest bucks I'd ever seen. Supposedly, a "friend" of his had killed both animals, but my client couldn't offer any other details. Although those bucks remained firmly implanted in my mind, further details continued to be unavailable for the next few years.

Then, in the early 1980s, I was fortunate to meet Fred Goodwin of Sherman Mills, Maine, one of America's foremost whitetail collectors. Fred had gathered more than 1,300 sets of antlers over a span of nearly 70 years, and along with these, he'd

Photo by Ron Brown

HOLE-IN-THE-HORN, OHIO, 1940

	Right Antler	Left Antler	Difference
Main Beam Length	25 5/8	24 4/8	1 1/8
1st Point Length	9 4/8	8 6/8	6/8
2nd Point Length	11 3/8	3 0/8	8 3/8
3rd Point Length	1 7/8	3 2/8	1 3/8
4th Point Length	–	–	–
5th Point Length	–	–	–
1st Circumference	6 2/8	5 6/8	4/8
2nd Circumference	5 0/8	4 6/8	2/8
3rd Circumference	7 5/8	5 1/8	2 4/8
4th Circumference	2 4/8	1 6/8	6/8
Total	69 6/8	56 7/8	15 5/8

Main Characteristics: Most whitetail experts believe this deer is the greatest non-typical of all time. It has an unbelievable 192 7/8" of abnormal points.

MISCELLANEOUS STATS	
No. Of Points–Right	23
No. Of Points–Left	22
Total No. Of Points	45
Length Of Abnormals	192 7/8
Greatest Spread	33 0/8
Tip To Tip Spread	21 2/8
Inside Spread	24 3/8

FINAL TALLY	
Inside Spread	24 3/8
Right Antler	69 6/8
Left Antler	56 7/8
Gross Score	151 0/8
Difference	-15 5/8
Subtotal	135 3/8
Abnormals	+192 7/8
NET NON-TYPICAL SCORE	328 2/8

acquired thousands of antler photos. As I dug through cigar and shoe boxes full of photos, one in particular caught my eye—a photo just like one of those I'd seen four years earlier around that campfire!

The inscription on the back of the photo, which was in Fred's handwriting, read, "giant non-typical found dead along railroad tracks, greatest spread 36 inches, 60 points, Kent, Ohio." I soon learned that Fred had acquired the photo several

years earlier from one of his many pen pals. Fred had never seen the buck, but he claimed it was the largest non-typical whitetail he knew of.

Eventually, I learned that the photo had come from a private hunting club in Kent, Ohio, and that the buck still hung in the bar there. In the summer of 1982, I talked with a couple of club members to learn more of this deer. Because of time and distance from my Montana home, however, it was actually August 1983 before I could travel to Kent to see the giant for myself.

By then, he'd hung in the smoke-filled bar for right at 40 years, and both the mount and antlers were nearly black from stains

This is the photo of the Hole-In-The-Horn that first tipped Dick Idol off to the existence of the gigantic non-typical, which he later uncovered in Kent, Ohio. Photo courtesy Dick Idol.

deer's background, I learned that he'd been found dead more than 40 years earlier and had hung in virtual seclusion ever since.

The Kent Canadian Club was founded in the early 1920s by

and dust. But, I immediately knew the antlers were of gigantic proportions and that they were even larger than they'd appeared in the photo. My initial rough score was off the "Richter Scale," at 349 2/8 Boone and Crockett points—well above that of the recently discovered 333 7/8-point world record from Missouri!

At the time of my visit, widespread interest in collecting whitetail racks was just beginning. I'd already acquired a substantial collection of outstanding bucks (many of which are featured in this book) and had begun displaying them at sportsmen's shows. The Kent Canadian Club was interested in making its giant buck more visible to the general public, and I eventually acquired the mounted head.

North American WHITETAIL magazine, which I had been involved with since I helped in its founding in 1982, also played an instrumental role in this saga. We shared a common goal of uncovering the origin and history of the buck and passing along that information to the hunting public. As I dug into the

a group of local hunters and fishermen who shared a special sporting interest in Ontario, Canada, and fellowship at their local clubhouse/bar in Kent. In the early days of the club, land was purchased at a site along the French River, where it joins Elephant Lake in Ontario. Later, a main lodge and cabins, bath houses, etc., were added, and it became the focal point of recreation for the membership. Because most of the membership lived near Kent, a clubhouse/bar was also established there. The club's 300 social members can use the local facility, but only the 20 "backroom" members are allowed to use the Ontario site.

One of the early members, Charlie Flowers, was an engineer for Erie Railroad Company of Ohio and apparently was directly responsible for the club's ownership of the rack. It's unclear whether Charlie was one of the individuals who found the deer or if he merely came into possession of the antlers from another person. Regardless, he ended up with the rack.

At the time I acquired the Hole-In-

The-Horn, the circumstances surrounding the buck's death and recovery were largely speculative. According to descendants of those involved and other information available then, the buck had been found dead along the railroad right-of-way near Windham, Ohio, in 1940 or shortly thereafter. The carcass was badly decomposed, so only the head was salvaged. It was believed that one of the engineers spotted the dead buck from the train itself

Can you imagine what this buck must have looked like on the hoof? Certainly, this is one of the most awesome bucks of all time. Photo by Dick Idol courtesy North American WHITETAIL.

and died from injuries, stress or starvation? And for that matter, on which side of the fence was he found? Apparently, nobody knew.

I was told that Charlie had sold the rack to the Kent Canadian Club for $25. The club then commissioned Ben Morgan, a taxidermist in nearby Akron, to acquire a new cape and mount the head. Once completed, it hung in the club's bar and essentially remained anonymous until I "discovered" it.

and at some point (then, or at a later date) recovered the antlers.

According to what I could learn at the time of my investigation, the buck had been found in or near the Ravenna Arsenal in Portage County. This arsenal is still used for storage of military munitions, and for security reasons, it's surrounded by a high fence. What nobody could tell me was whether or not the fence had played some role in the deer's death. Had the barrier caused him to become trapped, resulting in death by collision with the train? Or, had he perhaps become entangled in the fence itself

But, this was not just any deer hanging in a bar—he would have been the undisputed world record for 40 years!

Once the head arrived at my home, there was time for closer scrutiny and opportunity for more careful measuring. There was no doubt that the head would become either No. 1 or No. 2 in the B&C record book. The staff at *North American WHITETAIL* and I knew this buck was a world record contender, so we searched for a name that would give him his own identity. Because there was no hunter's name to attach to this deer, as there is with most other trophy heads, we had to find something else to call him.

At that time, perhaps the most mysterious aspect of this rack was the fact that one of the large drop tines on the right main beam had a small hole through it. There was a great deal of speculation as to how and when the hole was created, so we dubbed this awesome animal the "Hole-In-The-Horn Buck." That monicker has since become universally accepted.

From the first time I unofficially scored the head, I knew it was a measurer's nightmare, as it had configurations of antler never before encountered on any whitetail rack. There was obviously more than one interpretation of how it should be scored, but most of the net scores from my measurements and those of many experienced measurers fell somewhere in the 340s—usually between 342 and 349 points.

Based on these unofficial scores, we felt the probability was high that this buck's final score would exceed the 333 7/8-point score of the world record "St. Louis Buck," which had been found dead

The incredible overall mass of the Hole-In-The-Horn's antlers can only be fully appreciated when viewed from the side. Photo by Dick Idol courtesy North American WHITETAIL.

less than two years earlier. But, we also knew the margin was close enough that the official scoring for entry into the records should not be done by just any official measurer. We wanted it done by someone who was very experienced and well respected within B&C's ranks. No measurer fit this description better than Phil Wright, chairman of the Scoring Committee and one of the most senior members of the club.

On August 27, 1983, the head was taken to Phil for the official scoring. After long and careful examination, he arrived at an entry score of 342 3/8, well above the world record. Phil also stated at the time that two or three other abnormal points he hadn't included in the total possibly could be added in during a final scoring by B&C judges' panel. If these points were included, the final score would be close to 349 points, very near my initial net score.

Based upon Phil's official entry score, the December 1983 issue *North American WHITETAIL* announced the shocking news of this historic buck and published information on both his "discovery" and the recent scoring. The magazine called the buck a "new world record," because according to Phil's official entry score, he was indeed just that.

Just a year prior to the initial scoring of the Hole-In-The-Horn, the enormous buck found dead near St. Louis had been officially scored by B&C measurer Dean Murphy, who also worked for the Missouri Department of Conservation and was an official member of the Awards Program judges' panel. Based upon Dean's entry score of 325 3/8 points, the Missouri buck had been highly publicized by newspapers and sporting magazines (including *North American WHITETAIL)* as a "new world record."

When the St. Louis Buck had first been announced to the world, he wasn't yet an "official" world record, because he hadn't been verified as such by a panel of B&C measurers. He was to be remeasured in the spring of 1983, at which time a final decision on his score would be rendered. However, to my knowledge, there was no negative reaction to claiming this deer to be the next No.1 non-typical.

The announcement of the Hole-In-The-Horn Buck in *North American WHITETAIL* followed that precedent. According to an official score sheet filled out by Phil Wright, the Ohio buck was just as much a "new world record" as the Missouri buck had been the previous year, when all anyone had to go on was Dean's entry score.

Only a couple of months prior to my acquiring the Hole-In-The-Horn Buck, in the summer of 1983, B&C's 18th Awards Program was held. There, the official score of the Missouri buck was raised from 325 3/8 points to 333 7/8. At the time, this hardly seemed an issue, because either way, the score was far in excess of Jeff Benson's 286-point world record from Texas. But now, there was a new contender for that crown.

The next three-year scoring period culminated with the 19th Awards Program on June 28, 1986. Top recent entries in all big game categories were to be on hand for panel scoring and display. It was pointed out by B&C officials that should the Hole-In-The-Horn not appear, he'd be listed in the next record book with an asterisk, indicating that the score shown

Here's the famous hole in the horn from which the buck gets its name. In this story, the recently discovered answer to how the mysterious hole got there is revealed. Photo courtesy Dick Idol.

was still subject to verification by a judges' panel. What's more, we were told that the deer could be dropped from the record book at some point in the future if not panel-measured. Eager to have the score confirmed, I placed the Hole-In-The-Horn in the custody of Phil Wright for transportation to the Awards Program.

When the buck was remeasured by the panel, the original 5x5 typical frame was rejected and a 4x4 typical configuration chosen. The final score submitted by the panel was 328 2/8 points, and it wasn't subject to appeal. To everybody's surprise, the Hole-In-The-Horn had become the official No. 2 non-typical.

From the first announcement of the original entry score of this buck, there was in certain quarters criticism of claims that he was a new world record. This seemed strange to me at the time, and still does, because the first wave of publicity on the Hole-In-The-Horn was little different from that regarding the Missouri buck. When these deer were revealed to the public, neither was an "official" world record; however, each had been entered at a score that, if upheld, would make him one.

Whatever the motivations for downplaying the Ohio buck, the resulting con-

Official B&C scorer Phil Wright is pictured carrying out the daunting task of measuring the Hole-In-The-Horn as an anxious Dick Idol looks on. Photo courtesy Dick Idol.

fusion about which buck was actually "bigger" detracted from the fact that these two racks tower above all others as the largest of all time. Both the Hole-In-The-Horn and the St. Louis Buck are of a size that could hardly even have been imagined before they surfaced. Since the B&C record book had been founded, the Benson Buck from Texas had been the undisputed No. 1 non-typical. Then, out of the clear blue, within a couple of years of each other, two bucks that exceeded even the most optimistic dreams of the whitetail fraternity had come onto the scene. A new benchmark had been established.

Regardless of his final score, the Hole-In-The-Horn Buck is undeniably one of the two most awesome non-typicals of all time. Even though he looks huge in photos, they still don't reflect his true size. For example, photography can't indicate that even after 40 years of drying, the rack still weighs 11 1/2 pounds!

It's also worth noting that while phenomenal mass is what makes the Hole-In-The-Horn so impressive in the eyes of many experts, it actually contributes little to his final score. I think most whitetail aficionados who've seen both heads would concede that the Hole-In-The-Horn has more antler volume than any other buck in history, including the St. Louis Buck. On the other hand, the St. Louis non-typical has a lot of long points, and he apparently grew several more that broke off before he was found. So, the debate over which of these bucks is bigger undoubtedly will continue.

However, as of very recently, we're no longer in the dark as to what caused the unique antler feature that gave the Hole-In-The-Horn Buck his name. As noted, at the time I conducted my interviews and other research on the story of this buck (1983), about all that was known for certain was that a railroad man named Charlie Flowers had sold the antlers to the Kent Canadian Club and that taxidermist Ben Morgan had mounted the deer. After that story appeared in the December 1983 issue of *North American WHITETAIL*, we naturally hoped somebody out there might come forth with new information, but more than a decade passed without that happening.

Then, in 1995, *WHITETAIL* editor Gordon Whittington received a cryptic note with a Florida postmark. "For information on the Hole in Horn buck, contact me," it read. "I was present."

Well aware that all eyewitnesses to the recovery of this deer had supposedly been dead for many years, Gordon was understandably skeptical. But, he dialed the phone number on the card anyway, and in so doing, he took the first step toward solving the greatest mystery in whitetail history.

As it turned out, the person who'd sent the card—a 76-year-old gentleman named George Winters—had indeed seen the Hole-In-The-Horn Buck in the flesh. What's more, he'd apparently been the first human to touch that enormous right antler with the strange hole through it. And in so doing, he told Gordon that he'd seen with his own eyes what had caused the hole!

George recounted that back in the early 1940s, when he was in his early 20s, he worked on a maintenance crew inside the arsenal. One bitterly cold morning, he and another guy were riding along a road near the perimeter fence when they saw several railroad workers on the outside of the fence. The men had apparently come down from the railroad track, which was roughly 75 yards from the fence.

Eager to see what was going on, George and his companion parked and walked down to the fence. There, they found the railroad workers pulling on the body of a large animal, which was stuck under the barrier. Actually, the carcass was entirely outside of the fence but part of the rack was wedged beneath the wires.

"We didn't know what it was," George remembered. "One of the men said, 'It's an elk!' Then, another one said, 'No, it's a moose!' I'd seen deer before, but I really wasn't sure if this was one or not. The animal had been dead for a week or so, from the looks of it, and he was huge. He looked like he weighed 300 or 400 pounds. He'd obviously been hit by a train."

> *"We didn't know what it was," George remembered. "One of the men said, 'It's an elk!' Then, another one said, 'No, it's a moose!' I'd seen deer before, but I really wasn't sure if this was one or not."*

One of the railroad men—George never caught his name—announced that he wanted the antlers, and the crew started pulling the giant out from under the fence. But, the animal wouldn't come free. George noticed that when they pulled on the legs, the fence swayed. The rack itself was stuck.

George got a shovel and began working to free the right antler, which was solidly wedged under the wires. "It had been so cold that the ground was frozen down six or eight inches," George recalled. "That antler was actually frozen into the ground. The fence was made of chain link, and it had stiff wires sticking down along the bottom of it. When I finally got the rack free, I noticed one of those pieces of wire was sticking down through the antler!

"I guess for years everyone has been wondering what made that hole," George noted, "but it definitely was caused by that wire."

This all makes sense to me. There are several scratches around the hole, and its diameter is roughly the same as that of the wire used on chain-link fences. Because this drop tine is rather "porous" out near its tip, I have no trouble believing that a buck thrashing around in pain would be able to poke a stiff wire all the way through it.

So, there you have it—an unexpected eyewitness account of the recovery of what might well be the most legendary whitetail of all. Now, it seems, the book on this giant can be closed once and for all.

> *"The fence was made of chain link, and it had stiff wires sticking down along the bottom of it. When I finally got the rack free, I noticed one of those pieces of wire was sticking down through the antler!"*

Chapter Fifteen

THE ILLINOIS ROADKILL

176 5/8 TYPICAL, ILLINOIS, 1965

The Buck Too Big To Believe

BY DICK IDOL

The November night was cold, and a misty rain darkened it even more than normal. An unsuspecting motorist from Fort Madison, Iowa, traveled down Illinois Hwy. 96 about two miles east of the small town of Nauvoo in Randolph County. There was no hint of what was about to happen.

Suddenly, a large form came out of the ditch and onto the roadway. For the driver, there was no avoiding the collision and the impact was signaled by a solid thump. Another big buck had met his demise at the front end of a vehicle.

Not long afterwards, Illinois conservation officer Jim Twitchell was directed to pick up the road-killed deer. Jim and the others who saw the deer found themselves unable to believe the size of either the body or the rack. They were enormous!

From all accounts, the buck had a staggering live weight of over 400 pounds. After studying the accompanying newspaper photo (top of page 105) showing part of his body and head, I have no reason to doubt this weight.

The antlers certainly have shrunk some since the buck was hit that night back in 1965, but even now, the outside spread across the beams remains an unbelievable 31 inches. The buck's head was proportionate to his rack and body, and the distance between the antler burrs is 3 1/2 inches. That gap is one of the largest I've ever seen.

Although the body and skin are long since gone, the antlers remain as evidence of

Illinois Roadkill, 1965

	Right Antler	Left Antler	Difference
Main Beam Length	31 0/8	29 0/8	2 0/8
1st Point Length	5 0/8	5 3/8	3/8
2nd Point Length	13 4/8	13 2/8	2/8
3rd Point Length	12 1/8	11 5/8	4/8
4th Point Length	–	7 5/8	7 5/8
5th Point Length	–	–	–
1st Circumference	6 0/8	6 0/8	–
2nd Circumference	5 4/8	5 1/8	3/8
3rd Circumference	5 7/8	5 6/8	1/8
4th Circumference	5 4/8	5 4/8	–
Total	**84 4/8**	**89 2/8**	**11 2/8**

Main Characteristics: Tremendous spread and mass. Main frame is scored as a 4x4 with base typical score of 191 4/8.

MISCELLANEOUS STATS	
No. Of Points–Right	5
No. Of Points–Left	7
Total No. Of Points	12
Length Of Abnormals	14 7/8
Greatest Spread	31 0/8
Tip To Tip Spread	22 5/8
Inside Spread	29 0/8

FINAL TALLY	
Inside Spread	29 0/8
Right Antler	84 4/8
Left Antler	89 2/8
Gross Score	202 6/8
Difference	-11 2/8
Subtotal	191 4/8
Abnormals	-14 7/8
NET TYPICAL SCORE	**176 5/8**

what a great buck he was. Besides such spectacular dimensions and statistics as weighing 11 pounds and having a 31-inch spread, 6-inch bases, 29 and 31-inch main beams and 12 points, with any luck at all this rack could have been near the top of the record book. His left beam has five classic typical points, but instead of a typical G-4 (third primary) off the main beam on his right antler, this buck grew a third tine off the second primary (G-2), making it an abnormal deduction. If this point had grown off the main beam as a

typical tine, the Illinois giant's net typical score would have been over 20 points higher than it actually is—simply by moving one tine!

Because his right antler has only four typical points, the "Illinois Roadkill," as he is called, scores as a giant 8-pointer. From a scoring standpoint, he gets no credit for the extra typical point on the left beam (the 7 5/8-inch G-4 tine) because it doesn't have a mate on the right beam. Despite all of this, the buck has an unbelievable gross score of 202

6/8, which is unheard of for an 8-point typical. Unfortunately, when the abnormal points and side-to-side differences in symmetry are subtracted, he winds up with a net of 176 5/8. This is a respectable score that easily makes the B&C record book, but it hardly reflects the true size of the antlers. The truth is that many think this buck is one of the most impressive deer of all time. In person, he's almost too big to believe!

With the people as a frame of reference, this photo, taken soon after the buck was killed by a car, reveals the rack's true size. Photo courtesy Dick Idol.

Many years ago, I began realizing that more than a "fair share" of big bucks were being killed by vehicles on the highways. In fact, several I was hunting met their end while trying to cross roads. Similar stories also have been related to me by other hunters. If we consider the relatively small number of mature bucks in a population that also includes does, fawns and immature bucks, and then check the percentage of road-killed deer that are mature bucks, we realize that for some reason, trophy deer are killed by

Not only is this buck wide, 31 inches outside, look at the height of the antlers! Photo by Dick Idol.

vehicles more often, relatively speaking, than are does and smaller bucks. Why?

In the fall, as bucks become more excited about the upcoming breeding season, they gradually expand their range of travel. About this same time, farmers begin harvesting crops and hunters begin bowhunting, scouting, setting up stands, small-game hunting, etc. All of this activity makes mature bucks nervous, causing them to become even more nocturnal than usual. Now, with more area to cover and with fewer safe hours in which to cover it, big bucks often spend virtually all night on the move.

Many deer are road-killed because vehicle headlights blind and confuse them. So, because the mature bucks are traveling more than other segments of the deer population and these movements are concentrated at night, it makes sense that a greater percentage of these active bucks would be killed on the highways than is the case with the other types of deer.

When one of those old, mossy-racked giants does get killed on the road, it's usually a big topic of conversation among local folks. "I can't believe a buck that big even lived around here" or "I've never seen him before" are the usual lines. This just further verifies the nocturnal trademark and elusive capabilities of the modern mature buck.

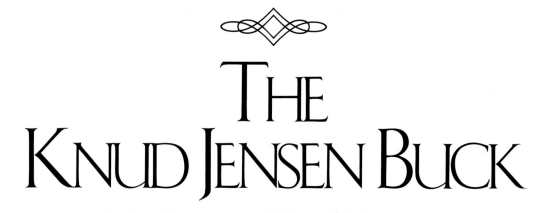

Chapter Sixteen

THE KNUD JENSEN BUCK

186 TYPICAL, MINNESOTA, 1955

The Swamp Buck Of The Great Northwoods

BY DICK IDOL

Knud Jensen and the saga of his giant buck from Erskin Swamp in north-ern Minnesota represent an era of deer hunting that is now little more than a memory…and a few nostalgic old photos. Knud's "deer" cabin, located 50 miles south of International Falls and the Canadian border, was a log cabin complete with stone fireplace and outdoor johns. It sat on a bench overlooking scenic Deer Lake, which connected to Pickerel and Battle lakes. This was the "wilds" of northern Minnesota, complete with bear, moose, deer, grouse and a variety of fishing that included walleye, perch, crappie and northern pike. It was a sportsman's paradise, and the setting measured up to that romantic image many of us envision as the great Northwoods.

This was raw wilderness that was not well suited for the faint-hearted hunter. There was no farmland and precious few roads. During the heart of the November deer season, the snow was often deep and the mercury frequently dropped to 30 below zero or colder. To venture into Erskin Swamp for a day of hunting was more

Main Characteristics: Outside spread is over 30", as are both main beams.

KNUD JENSEN, MINNESOTA, 1955

	Right Antler	Left Antler	Difference
Main Beam Length	30 5/8	31 3/8	6/8
1st Point Length	8 2/8	7 1/8	1 1/8
2nd Point Length	11 0/8	10 5/8	3/8
3rd Point Length	10 7/8	12 4/8	1 5/8
4th Point Length	8 2/8	6 4/8	1 6/8
5th Point Length	–	–	–
1st Circumference	5 1/8	5 0/8	1/8
2nd Circumference	4 4/8	4 4/8	–
3rd Circumference	5 0/8	5 0/8	–
4th Circumference	4 6/8	4 5/8	1/8
Total	**88 3/8**	**87 2/8**	**5 7/8**

MISCELLANEOUS STATS	
No. Of Points–Right	5
No. Of Points–Left	9
Total No. Of Points	14
Length Of Abnormals	10 1/8
Greatest Spread	30 6/8
Tip To Tip Spread	22 3/8
Inside Spread	26 3/8

FINAL TALLY	
Inside Spread	26 3/8
Right Antler	88 3/8
Left Antler	87 2/8
Gross Score	202 0/8
Difference	-5 7/8
Subtotal	196 1/8
Abnormals	-10 1/8
NET TYPICAL SCORE	186 0/8

than an adventure; it was a grueling experience wrought with a fair share of danger. Such was the setting in the November 1955 deer season when Knud Jensen met up with friends Dick Doyle and Nick Gentlle at their Northwoods deer camp.

Knud Jensen was a fairly heavy big man around 70 years old at the time. On this particular November hunt, two to three feet of powder was on the ground and the temperature was well below zero. With conditions so tough, this was not a day to hunt Erskin Swamp, which hap-

pened to be their favorite hunting grounds.

A couple of miles from the camp was an old logging road that twisted its way through patches of tamarack swamp and eventually dead-ended at a well-used deer run. Since walking was so tough in the deep snow, as they left the cabin at dawn, the three men decided that Knud would sit on the deer run at the end of the logging road. Dick and Nick would hunt another area in a different direction.

While there were few other hunters around in those days, there was one small group of guys that always hunted the same general area. So when Dick and Nick heard shots from Knud's direction, they weren't sure who was doing the shooting.

They kept hunting until late morning, when they happened to meet another hunter. He informed them that their "buddy down the old logging road had shot a hellava buck and wasn't having much luck getting it out." Immediately, Dick and Nick set out to find Knud.

They found the big man and immediately saw that the hunter they'd met was right. He was laboring to drag a huge buck in the deep snow and was more than glad to see his friends come to his rescue.

With an outside spread of 30 6/8 inches, Knud Jensen knew his big whitetail was remarkable even back in 1955. Photo courtesy Dick Doyle.

This group of friends had hunted together for years, and friendly ribbing was part of the tradition. Dick immediately shouted to Knud as they were approaching, "There goes my hunting for the day!" He was only kidding, of course, but it turned out to be the truth.

Knud had killed his buck on the edge of Erskin Swamp, and he was truly one of those legendary "swamp" bucks. His body was huge. All three men struggled most of the day to get the buck to a place they could reach with the truck.

The buck's body size was impressive, but it was nothing compared to the rack. Today, 40 years after the buck was shot,

the greatest spread is still an incredible 30 6/8 inches. In all likelihood when the buck was killed, he was over 33 inches wide! Both main beams are well over 30 inches, one still taping 31 3/8 inches. Few bucks in the world have the stats of 30x30x30, meaning both main beams and the outside spread top 30 inches. Numbers are just numbers, but what they define here is an incredible rack.

A 186 typical score is impressive, but it certainly doesn't paint a picture that represents the true appearance of this buck. He happens to fall victim to the "seam" in the scoring system — he has too many deductions from abnormal points (four on the left side) for the score to reflect his true size as a typical and not enough abnormals for a great non-typical score. Without those four abnormal points, he's almost a 200-class typical, a score more befitting his appearance.

Today, Knud's cabin still overlooks Deer Lake, but now the hunters are plenty and the land is largely tamed. Erskin Swamp and all the lakes and forests are still there, but Knud Jensen and the mystery and serenity of the great Northwoods of yesteryear have faded from memory. At least the story of Knud's hunt and his great buck are still with us to serve as a tribute to and reminder of a time gone by.

Chapter Seventeen

THE DELMER JOHNSON BUCK

230 6/8 NON-TYPICAL, ALBERTA, 1973

A 10-Minute Hunt To Legendary Fame

BY GREG MILLER

As one might imagine, the stories of how some of the "legendary whitetails" were taken are as different as the deer themselves. In some cases, the hunter may have had to overcome much adversity and travel long distances before tagging his trophy. Other stories highlight the great amount of time put forth by the successful hunters. In Delmer Johnson's story, however, an exhausting pursuit far away from home certainly wasn't required. You see, his hunt for the buck of a lifetime took place just outside his hometown and encompassed a grand total of 10 minutes on-stand.

Delmer lived in the town of Sylvan Lake, located in central Alberta approximately nine miles west of Red Deer and a mere 50 miles east of the Rocky Mountains. The terrain in this part of the province is a mixture of cropland and rather expansive chunks of "bush." As one might expect, there are good numbers of whitetail deer in the area. Moose, elk and mule deer also are quite common in this part of the province.

Main Characteristics: Massive non-typical with a total of 30 scorable points.

Delmer Johnson, Alberta, 1973

	Right Antler	Left Antler	Difference
Main Beam Length	27 5/8	27 2/8	3/8
1st Point Length	6 0/8	7 3/8	1 3/8
2nd Point Length	12 3/8	11 3/8	1 0/8
3rd Point Length	10 5/8	5 4/8	5 1/8
4th Point Length	7 0/8	8 0/8	1 0/8
5th Point Length	–	–	–
1st Circumference	5 7/8	6 0/8	1/8
2nd Circumference	5 5/8	5 1/8	4/8
3rd Circumference	5 3/8	6 3/8	1 0/8
4th Circumference	5 7/8	7 0/8	1 1/8
Total	**86 3/8**	**84 0/8**	**11 5/8**

Miscellaneous Stats	
No. Of Points–Right	14
No. Of Points–Left	16
Total No. Of Points	30
Length Of Abnormals	52 5/8
Greatest Spread	29 0/8
Tip To Tip Spread	9 7/8
Inside Spread	19 3/8

Final Tally	
Inside Spread	19 3/8
Right Antler	86 3/8
Left Antler	84 0/8
Gross Score	**189 6/8**
Difference	-11 5/8
Subtotal	178 1/8
Abnormals	+52 5/8
Net Non-Typical Score	**230 6/8**

In early November 1973, Delmer embarked on his fateful hunt. He already had a game plan figured out for this particular day. Delmer knew of a large barley field west of Sylvan Lake that was surrounded by a chunk of heavy cover. He suspected it would be the perfect place to try and ambush a big buck, but not just any big buck. During the previous deer season, Delmer had seen a giant buck in the field. And just before the season opened this year, he had seen what he thought was the same big buck not far from the field.

Weather conditions were far from ideal for a deer hunt on the chosen day. The temperature was well below the freezing mark, and snow was falling hard. Despite the conditions, Delmer made his way to the stand site he had selected. A bit of inclement weather wasn't going to deter the veteran trapper and hunter from sticking to his plan of attack.

Prior to making his hunt, Delmer had scouted the area and had discovered something quite interesting. The farmer who had harvested the crop of barley had left behind a pile of grain in the middle of the field. A quick look was all it took to show Delmer that a good number of deer were feeding on the pile of discarded barley. Delmer figured maybe one of those deer was the big buck he had seen in the area on two previous occasions.

By the time Delmer got settled into his stand along the edge of the field, it was already 8 a.m. Although his set-up would allow him to remain well-hidden, he was able to see the pile of barley and most of the big field. All that was left was to make himself comfortable for what might well turn out to be a long wait. However, as he was about to find out, the wait would be a short one today.

Ten minutes after getting settled, Delmer noticed some movement about 150 yards away in the timber along the edge of the field. Turning his attention to that spot, he strained his eyes to better see through the falling snow. Suddenly, a big buck walked out into the barley field and stopped. Even though the animal was facing him, Delmer didn't hesitate a bit. He lined up his sights on the monster deer and squeezed off a shot from his .308 Savage lever-action rifle. The bullet struck the buck squarely in the chest, dropping him on the spot.

Even before he left his stand, Delmer knew the buck was big but the heavy snowfall had made it difficult to tell just how big. It wasn't until he was actually standing over the fallen animal that he realized just how large the deer truly was. Not only did the buck possess a huge set of antlers, he also had a gigantic body. Delmer found out just how heavy the buck was when it came time to load him into his pickup truck. After struggling with the dead animal a while, he finally decided the only way he was

going to get the huge buck loaded by himself was by cutting him in half.

As stated earlier, Delmer Johnson had been a trapper and hunter all his life. He had killed many large bucks. Maybe that's why he initially had no intentions of having his 1973 kill measured for the record book. Luckily, an old friend of the family, Gerry Smith of Eckville, Alberta, saw Delmer's trophy and coaxed him into having the antlers scored.

The inside spread of the Johnson Buck is 19 3/8 inches; however, the greatest spread reaches out to a whopping 29 inches! There are 14 scorable points on the right beam and 16 on the left. Main beam lengths are 27 5/8 and 27 2/8 inches. Circumference measurements at the bases are 5 7/8 and 6 inches. When all the numbers are tallied, the 30-point monster winds up scoring 230 6/8 net non-typical. (The huge rack has that massive, gnarly, multi-tined build that truly epitomizes trophy Canadian whitetails.)

Thanks in part to Gerry Smith, the Johnson Buck eventually garnered the attention it rightly deserved. The deer won the Grand Champion Award for the best whitetail in Alberta for 1973. And at the time it was taken, the buck also ranked as the best non-typical whitetail ever from the province. Although it has since lost its No.1 provincial ranking, the buck is still among the top five from Alberta.

As most whitetail aficionados can attest, stories about deer of this caliber are rare, but to take such a buck on a 10-minute hunt …well, that's unheard of! But, that's the beauty of trophy whitetail hunting—even when you're behind, it doesn't take long to catch up!

Chapter Eighteen

THE MEL JOHNSON BUCK

204 4/8 TYPICAL, ILLINOIS, 1965

Archery's Undisputed World Record Typical

BY JACK EHRESMAN

Stories of record-book deer make good reading, particularly when they're twisted around a horseback ride into the wilderness, fresh snow on the tents and the aroma of coffee over a snapping campfire. But, successful hunts don't always unfold in such romantic settings. A trophy buck also can dwell in a patch of timber close to your back door.

Mel Johnson, a big, broad-shouldered bowhunter, learned this fact a long time ago in his native Illinois, a state with plenty of farming, industry and big deer. The year was 1965, and the setting was the edge of a small soybean field near a busy state highway only 15 minutes from Mel's home in Peoria.

Although the hunt didn't occur in an exotic location, the end result remains the envy of every hunter who has ever challenged these magnificent animals. Mel's buck scored 204 4/8 typical points and, at this writing, remains the only North American big game animal ever to receive both the coveted Ishi and Sagamore Hill awards, the highest recognition bestowed upon big game hunters by the Pope and Young and Boone and Crockett clubs, respectively.

Mel had six years' experience and about that many deer to his credit when confronted with his golden opportunity. He and hunting buddy Bill Kallister had seen several large deer on a certain farm during the 1964 season, so they obtained permis-

MEL JOHNSON, ILLINOIS, 1965

	Right Antler	Left Antler	Difference
Main Beam Length	27 5/8	26 6/8	7/8
1st Point Length	5 4/8	7 2/8	1 6/8
2nd Point Length	11 3/8	12 0/8	5/8
3rd Point Length	12 6/8	12 0/8	6/8
4th Point Length	10 1/8	9 7/8	2/8
5th Point Length	5 7/8	4 4/8	1 3/8
1st Circumference	6 1/8	6 2/8	1/8
2nd Circumference	5 0/8	5 0/8	—
3rd Circumference	5 1/8	5 1/8	—
4th Circumference	4 6/8	5 1/8	3/8
Total	**94 2/8**	**93 7/8**	**6 1/8**

Main Characteristics: World record typical bow kill. Gross typical score 211 6/8.

MISCELLANEOUS STATS

No. Of Points–Right	7
No. Of Points–Left	6
Total No. Of Points	13
Length Of Abnormals	1 1/8
Greatest Spread	26 1/8
Tip To Tip Spread	22 5/8
Inside Spread	23 5/8

FINAL TALLY

Inside Spread	23 5/8
Right Antler	94 2/8
Left Antler	93 7/8
Gross Score	**211 6/8**
Difference	-6 1/8
Subtotal	205 5/8
Abnormals	-1 1/8
NET TYPICAL SCORE	**204 4/8**

sion to hunt there in 1965.

When season arrived, it didn't take long before they knew a giant buck was around. Mel actually spotted him twice, but each time, he was too far away. Knowing what was near, both archers passed up shots on smaller deer early on.

On this particular Friday, Mel went to the field alone, as Bill had to work late. Mel had been using stands that would allow shots well out into the field. Now, however, he decided to change tactics and take a ground stand, from which he could watch the edge of the timber instead of only the field.

That fateful afternoon, Mel found a brushy spot and settled in. The wind was blowing from the woods across the field—perfect. Sure enough, the bowhunter soon noticed a deer stepping from the timber at the upper corner of the field, about 300 yards away. It was a huge buck, standing motionless, scenting and looking over the open field before taking another step.

Mel's adrenaline began to pump as the massive animal, his large antlers swinging in rhythm with each cautious step, started working his way across the upper end of the field. Eventually, the buck made it across the field and turned toward Mel's position. The hunter now noticed a dryness in his mouth, and his heart really began to pound. Mel realized that if the buck continued on his present course, eventually he'd wind up right in his lap!

"Several times in the past, I had things happen that spooked deer, like a quick change in the wind direction or perhaps a slight movement on my part," Mel said. "I didn't want it to happen this time, so I kept hugging the concealment of my blind."

This time, the wind remained in Mel's favor, and the buck never changed direction. Soon, the huge deer was within 30 yards. The spread of the antlers was breathtaking. Mel swallowed to avoid coughing and moved his right leg slightly to relieve a cramp.

The buck continued toward the archer, who suddenly realized the brute was now too close. "I was pinned down and couldn't rise to try a shot. At that close range, he would see me and be off like a flash. I decided to wait, let him get by me and gamble on a shot going away.

"He was about three or four rows into the bean field," Mel added. "At one time, when he was only about 20 yards away, we stared at each other for what seemed like an eternity. Eventually, he swung his head to scan the open field and started moving again."

That's when Mel went into action. He rose quickly from his stand, drawing his 72-pound recurve in the same motion. The left-handed shooter let an arrow fly; the buck jumped and raced a short distance to the middle of the open field

before pausing on a ridge, watching the hunter. The deer seemed curious as to what had happened. Then, he turned and again ran from Mel's sight.

When the bowhunter next spotted the buck, he was lying on the ground, kicking his last. En route, Mel found his arrow intact on the ground. It had passed completely through the deer, which had never made it out of the bean field.

Mel tried to drag the huge buck from the field but couldn't budge him. Fortunately, the farmer offered a hand, and the deer was soon secured across the top of Mel's car trunk.

"Back then, little was mentioned about trophy racks," Mel recalled. "I found out about Boone and Crockett through a clipping in a magazine. I wrote to them, and they sent me the name of the only official measurer in the state, a man at the Museum of Natural History in Chicago."

About that time, Mel also purchased a book on measuring and scoring antlers. He then drove to Chicago to have his deer officially measured. There, the buck was scored at a net of slightly more than 197 typical. This puzzled Mel somewhat since, using his book as a reference, he had come up with a "green" score of around 207. Inspecting the official score sheet, he saw that one of the circumference figures had been omitted. A judges' panel eventually gave him a final score of 204 4/8, making it the undisputed archery world record even until today!

"It was just luck. That's what it amounts to," said Mel. "I guess the whole thing is being able to hold your composure when you get such an opportunity. That's the difference between getting a big deer and not getting one."

Chapter Nineteen

THE
JAMES JORDAN BUCK

206 1/8 TYPICAL, WISCONSIN, 1914

The World Record Over
50 Years In The Making

BY DICK IDOL

For some reason, the stories of high-ranking whitetails often involve bizarre circumstances. The tale of James (Jim) Jordan's amazing typical from Wisconsin is no exception. In fact, it could be argued that this is the strangest whitetail story of all.

Accounts of the hunt, as told by Jim before his death, have been printed in various publications, and these are apparently the only sources of factual information since all of the other participants and eyewitnesses have long since passed on. Based on these materials, what follows is the story of a chain of unlikely events that spanned 64 years and eventually led to the recognition of Jim's massive 10-pointer as the world's greatest typical whitetail.

It all began in the predawn of November 20, 1914, as Jim and friend Egus Davis readied their rented horse and wagon for a day of serious deer hunting. The new

JAMES JORDAN, WISCONSIN, 1914

	Right Antler	Left Antler	Difference
Main Beam Length	30 0/8	30 0/8	–
1st Point Length	7 6/8	7 3/8	3/8
2nd Point Length	13 0/8	13 1/8	1/8
3rd Point Length	10 0/8	10 4/8	4/8
4th Point Length	6 0/8	7 5/8	1 5/8
5th Point Length	–	–	–
1st Circumference	6 2/8	6 1/8	1/8
2nd Circumference	6 2/8	6 4/8	2/8
3rd Circumference	7 3/8	7 4/8	1/8
4th Circumference	7 0/8	6 7/8	1/8
Total	93 5/8	95 5/8	3 2/8

Main Characteristics: The most famous 5x5 of all time. Tremendous mass and balance. Average circumference is 6 6/8". World record typical for 80 years.

MISCELLANEOUS STATS

No. Of Points–Right	5
No. Of Points–Left	5
Total No. Of Points	10
Length Of Abnormals	–
Greatest Spread	23 6/8
Tip To Tip Spread	7 5/8
Inside Spread	20 1/8

FINAL TALLY

Inside Spread	20 1/8
Right Antler	93 5/8
Left Antler	95 5/8
Gross Score	209 3/8
Difference	-3 2/8
Subtotal	206 1/8
Abnormals	–
NET TYPICAL SCORE	206 1/8

snow would make for good tracking, so expectations were high as the men bounced their way toward the Yellow River, where it snaked alongside the Soo Line Railroad just south of Danbury, Wisconsin.

Shortly after dawn, Egus bagged a fat doe. Winter meat was what he wanted, and this doe surely would be tastier than a tough, rutting buck. After borrowing Jim's knife to field-dress the doe, Egus suggested they load her onto the wagon and head for the house. But, Jim was a diehard and decided to keep hunting alone.

After Egus had left, Jim quietly began walking toward the river, keeping a sharp eye out for deer and fresh sign. Soon, he came upon furrows in the snow where several whitetails had meandered past. As he leaned over for a closer look at the obviously fresh tracks, what really caught his eye was the enormous size of one of the sets of hoofprints. Jim knew that tracks don't always indicate the size of a rack, but he couldn't help visualizing a huge set of antlers belonging to the buck that had left those nearly elk-sized prints. He had to follow them.

Jim easily tracked the group in the new snow as they meandered alongside the railroad tracks. Then, as the hunter paused to listen to the familiar whistle of

A rare photo of James Jordan with his buck, taken just before his death and before he was officially credited as having shot the world record typical. Photo courtesy North American WHITETAIL.

the train, the shrill scream caused four deer to come to their feet in the weeds just ahead of him. One of them was the biggest buck Jim had ever seen.

Instinctively, Jim shouldered his .25/20 Winchester and carefully aimed at the giant's neck. The rack was frozen in place as the deer, unaware of the hunter's presence, listened to the sounds of the approaching train. Posed against the blue sky of a clear, cold day, the majestic buck with his heavy, golden-brown rack left an impression Jim would never forget. Finally, the hunter squeezed off the shot. Deer scattered at the sound, does in one direction and the buck in the other. Jim fired until his magazine was empty as the racing buck made for nearby cover.

Even though the buck hadn't shown any visual signs of being hit, Jim felt certain he had connected with one or more shots. Now the hunter excitedly began following the long, leaping strides. But after going just a short distance, he realized his gun was empty. Only after a frantic search through all of his pockets did he discover a single remaining cartridge. This one would have to count!

Jim cautiously moved along the bounding tracks as they snaked through the thick brush toward the river. Finally, he saw what he had been looking for —

blood. It wasn't much, but it did verify he'd hit the buck.

Eventually, the huge animal slowed. At first, he afforded Jim only an occasional glimpse, but after a while, the hunter got to where he could stay in constant visual contact. However, Jim was not yet close enough to be sure of a finishing shot. Stumbling, the buck finally made it to the river, at a point only a few hundred yards from Jim's farm. It appeared he would stop, but suddenly, he jumped into the shallow river and made his way to the other side, surging through the light current.

By now, Jim had made his way to the river and was ready when the buck stepped from the water on the opposite bank. Still alert, the huge whitetail stared back across the river at his pursuer. Knowing his rifle was on the light side for such a big deer, Jim decided his best target would be the backbone. He took careful aim through the iron sights.

At the crack of the rifle, the huge buck folded. Jim immediately waded into the icy water, keeping an anxious eye on his prize. Now, after several distant glimpses, he could get a close look at those magnificent antlers and the immense body. He wasn't disappointed! The rack had 10 long, thick points and massive main beams, and the buck had a body to match. Estimates of the live weight were around 400 pounds.

Thinking he should field-dress the buck, Jim felt over the empty knife case

> *"At the crack of the rifle, the huge buck folded. Jim immediately waded into the icy water, keeping an anxious eye on his prize. Now, after several distant glimpses, he could get a close look at those magnificent antlers and the immense body. He wasn't disappointed!"*

and realized he had loaned the blade to Egus. It was cold, however, so it wouldn't hurt to leave the buck ungutted while Jim hiked the quarter-mile back to the farm to get his knife.

He could hardly contain his excitement when he found Egus and told him the whole story. Anxiously, they made their way back to the river to retrieve Jim's trophy—only to find the deer was gone! In a panic, they analyzed the situation and realized the buck must have given one last kick and slid into the river. Sure enough, at the first bend downriver, the big whitetail was found lodged on a rock in midstream. Once again, Jim waded through the frigid, waist-deep water to retrieve his prize.

Being a woodsman was a way of life for Jim. He'd fished, farmed, trapped and hunted as far back as he could remember. He was at home in the haunts of the whitetail and had taken many nice bucks. But, none was as large as this spectacular deer, so he decided to have the great trophy mounted.

One of the admirers who came to see the deer was a part-time taxidermist by the name of George VanCastle, who lived in the nearby town of Webster and worked on the Soo Railroad Line. Accepting an offer to mount the trophy for $5, Jim turned the unskinned head over to George, who left Danbury with it on the railroad, bound for Webster. As his buck left Danbury, little did Jim know that he wouldn't see him again for more than 50 years!

As fate would have it, George's wife became ill and died soon after he picked up the rack, prompting his decision to move to Hinckley, Minnesota. Several months later, Jim became concerned about the mount and traveled to Webster, only to discover that George had moved.

The air distance from Danbury to Hinckley was only 25 miles, but between the towns was a bridgeless stretch of the St. Croix River, making the trip difficult at best. For a variety of reasons, Jim postponed that trip to Hinckley until some time later, when a bridge finally had been constructed. Tragically, when Jim got to Hinckley, he learned that George had remarried, moved to Florida and presumably had taken the mounted head with him.

In reality, the mounted buck had never left Hinckley; it was stored in the attic of George's old house, where it continued to gather dust in obscurity. Even more ironically, Jim and his wife, Lena, moved to Hinckley several years after the deer was shot, where Jim operated a tav-

ern on the east side of town. His mounted head was stored right there in the same small town for years, and he never knew it! It was just another quirk in a long string of bizarre events in this melodrama.

A lot of years passed before this enormous mount mysteriously showed up at a rummage sale in Sandstone, Minnesota, in 1958. According to Robert "Bob" Ludwig, a Department of Natural Resources forest technician from Sandstone, the antlers were then black with age, the mount was held together with old twine and sawdust leaked from various openings. However, Bob was impressed with the massive antlers and figured they were worth the asking price of $3, so he sprang for it.

After his purchase, the mounted head was moved between storage in his house and the barn, depending on the particular mood of Bob's wife, who wasn't really all that impressed with his great "deal." Then, in 1964, Bob read an article in an outdoor magazine that described the method used by the Boone and Crockett

The most outstanding features of the Jordan Buck are mass and symmetry. Photo by Dick Idol.

123

Club to measure whitetail racks. Bob rough measured his rummage sale special at a net score of 205 B&C points, which would make the massive 10-pointer a new world record!

Presuming he'd made a mistake, Bob mailed his completed score sheet to Bernie Fashingbauer, an official B&C scorer and a director of the Science Museum of Minnesota's Lee and Rose Warner Nature Center. After a phone conversation, Bob was supposed to arrange a date for Bernie to score the trophy. However, nearly a year went by with no action.

But, then came another stroke of luck, this one good: While Bernie was on a hunting trip to the Sandstone area, he recognized Bob's name on a mailbox and decided to stop in. He'd indeed found the right person and after scoring the head tallied a potential world record score of 206 6/8 net points.

Then in 1971, the "Sandstone Buck," as he'd been dubbed, was sent to Pennsylvania, where he was rescored by a B&C judges' panel. The deer was indeed declared a new world record with a final net score of 206 1/8 points.

But still, there remained the question of whether or not the deer had been shot, and if so, by whom. In yet another strange twist, sometime after the initial scoring in 1964, Bob had met with his long-distant cousin—Jim Jordan!—to show off his incredible find. Immediately, Jim claimed this was the deer he'd shot way back in 1914!

Bob wasn't convinced, however, because he'd always been under the impression that Jim's rack had had a bullet hole in it. There was no hole in either of these antlers. Also, aside from Jim, there were no living witnesses who'd actually seen his deer. The debate continued for the next several years, as Jim tried to convince B&C officials and others that he'd indeed killed the buck a half-century prior. Meanwhile, in 1968, Dr. Charles Arnold purchased the rack from Bob for $1,500.

The question of whether the buck was from Minnesota or Wisconsin, and whether or not Jim was the hunter, endured for years. Finally, several persons, including Bernie Fashingbauer, Dr. Arnold and others, brought forth enough evidence to convince a B&C committee to accept Jim Jordan as the hunter and Danbury, Wisconsin, as the location of the kill.

By now, more than a decade had passed since Jim had first seen his buck's antlers again. During that interim, he'd gone to great lengths to convince people it was the same deer he'd shot so many years earlier but he'd continued to run into dead ends. Among all of the persons who'd seen the animal back in 1914, only he was still living. Jim wasn't interested in money; he merely wanted the recognition he felt was due him for having shot such a trophy.

Finally, in December 1978, Jim was declared the "hunter" of the world record

> *"Finally, in December 1978, Jim was declared the 'hunter' of the world-record typical. But in the strangest and most tragic of all twists in this saga, the hunter never got to hear his name announced. Two months prior to this historic decision by B&C, Jim died at the age of 86."*

typical. But in the strangest and most tragic of all twists in this saga, the hunter never got to hear his name announced. Two months prior to this historic decision by B&C, Jim died at the age of 86.

As you might expect of a deer that held the No. 1 position in the record book for almost a quarter-century (until Saskatchewan's Hanson Buck beat him out), the Jordan Buck is both huge and symmetrical. In fact, while the Hanson Buck is exceptionally well-balanced from one antler to the other, the Jordan Buck is even more so, with side-to-side differences of only 3 2/8 inches total. The buck's net score of 206 1/8 is a full 98.4 percent of his gross typical score, which is unmatched by any other whitetail in the upper tier of the record book. And, it shouldn't be overlooked that this deer achieved his phenomenal score as a straight 5x5!

Perhaps the most unusual characteristic of the Wisconsin rack is that it's so big and massive without having any abnormal points. This is the rarest of all traits in a truly world-class whitetail, for almost all of the great deer have at least one non-typical point. No matter where the Jordan Buck eventually ends up in the rankings, he'll always be regarded as one of the most massive, perfect and, yes, legendary of all deer.

Jim would certainly be proud.

> *"Perhaps the most unusual characteristic of the Wisconsin rack is that it's so big and massive without having any abnormal points. This is the rarest of all traits in a truly world-class whitetail, for almost all of the great deer have at least one non-typical point."*

Chapter Twenty

THE DAVID KLEMN BUCK

243 3/8 NON-TYPICAL, OHIO, 1980

Crab-Claw Giant Of The Suburbs

BY DICK IDOL

Ohio has long been recognized as one of the top big deer producers in North America. This fact has always amazed me because of its intense hunting pressure and relatively heavy human population, a scenario that generally equates to lots of young bucks and few trophy animals. Somehow, however, Ohio has been and still remains an exception to the rule.

This point struck me as far back as 1981, when I interviewed David Klemn for the story of his giant non-typical he'd taken the previous season. David lives in Mahoning County near Youngstown, Ohio, in what the residents there call the "country" but what more accurately might be described as "suburban countryside." There is a high density of homes and people living in the area.

To me, the story of his buck is a classic and truly points out the whitetail's unique ability to literally live right alongside man. During the summer of 1980, David watched a group of seven bachelor bucks living in a small swamp near his home. The area of cover was less that a mile across and was literally ringed by homes and vari-

DAVID KLEMN, OHIO, 1980

	Right Antler	Left Antler	Difference
Main Beam Length	27 7/8	29 7/8	2 0/8
1st Point Length	11 7/8	12 2/8	3/8
2nd Point Length	12 7/8	11 2/8	1 5/8
3rd Point Length	10 0/8	14 4/8	4 4/8
4th Point Length	11 7/8	12 4/8	5/8
5th Point Length	–	–	–
1st Circumference	4 5/8	4 6/8	1/8
2nd Circumference	4 4/8	4 5/8	1/8
3rd Circumference	5 6/8	7 0/8	1 2/8
4th Circumference	6 3/8	4 6/8	1 5/8
Total	**95 6/8**	**101 4/8**	**12 2/8**

Main Characteristics: Crab-claw appearance on tips of main beams. All typical tines are over 10" long! Brow tines are 11 7/8" and 12 2/8".

MISCELLANEOUS STATS	
No. Of Points–Right	11
No. Of Points–Left	9
Total No. Of Points	20
Length Of Abnormals	40 4/8
Greatest Spread	26 1/8
Tip To Tip Spread	1 4/8
Inside Spread	17 7/8

FINAL TALLY	
Inside Spread	17 7/8
Right Antler	95 6/8
Left Antler	101 4/8
Gross Score	215 1/8
Difference	-12 2/8
Subtotal	202 7/8
Abnormals	+40 4/8
NET NON-TYPICAL SCORE	**243 3/8**

ous businesses. That this small but thick area was home to at least seven bucks was unusual enough, but even more amazing was the fact that all seven of them were big! In fact, three of them were record class!

David had seen them on several occasions throughout the summer and felt sure they would still be there when the season rolled around. He planned to make an all out effort to get one of them. Having hunted there before, he knew the area well.

When opening morning finally rolled around, David took up a position on a well-used trail with his 12-gauge shotgun in hand just as daylight was breaking. Unconventional bucks often call for unorthodox tactics, and David had just the plan. At a predetermined time, his wife and kids would move toward him in the fashion of a tiger hunt, noisily clanging pots with spoons. They began on the opposite side of the swamp in hopes of moving the bucks down the run where David was waiting.

It wasn't long after he'd heard the first metallic clang in the distance that he also heard water sloshing and limbs breaking. He got ready. The first thing he saw was antlers moving above the low brush. By the time he got his 12 gauge to his shoulder, the buck was barrelling past. A well-placed slug dropped the buck on the spot.

As he walked up to the deer, he immediately recognized the huge, uniquely shaped rack as belonging to one of the three record-class bucks in the group of seven. This buck was especially memorable because of the basket shape of the beams, the exceptionally long 12-inch brow tines and the crossing of the main beams in the front, giving the appearance of

crab-like claws on each side. He was a tremendous buck, with main beams of 29 7/8 and 27 7/8 inches, an outside spread of 26 1/8 inches, a total of 20 points and tremendous mass throughout the rack. He ended up with a final score of 243 3/8 non-typical!

As a stated earlier, I was amazed when I actually saw the swamp where the buck was killed. If I had been living there and hadn't known better, I would have never given a second thought to hunting there. Obviously, neither did a lot of other hunters!

The real kicker, however, is that David swears that the other two big bucks in the group were noticeable bigger than his giant "Crab-Claw Buck," as he has come to be known. And, David Klemn is not a fellow prone to exaggeration.

The huge size of the base typical frame of non-typicals is often overlooked. The Crab-Claw Buck sports a gross typical frame scoring a whopping 215 1/8. Photo by Dick Idol.

Chapter Twenty-One

THE ELBURN KOHLER BUCK

265 3/8 NON-TYPICAL, SASKATCHEWAN, 1957

The Far North's "King Of White-Tailed Bucks"

BY ROB WEGNER

The Canadian province of Saskatchewan is a relatively flat, low-lying territory of over 250,000 square miles. Here, the plains or Dakota white-tailed deer *(Odocoileus virginianus dakotensis)* is distributed throughout the province. This province has recently emerged as a legendary name in trophy whitetail hunting, having produced such remarkable animals as the Garvey Buck and the Milo Hanson Buck. Indeed, Saskatchewan is perhaps the greatest producer of record whitetails in the world.

In looking through *Henry Kelsey's Big Game Records,* published by the Saskatchewan Wildlife Federation, one observes that the great bulk of the trophies were taken during the late 1950s and the 1960s, when hunters were fewer, pressure was lower and ideal habitat was in great abundance.

One of these bucks was shot on November 1, 1957, by a deer hunter named Elburn Kohler. This massive 33-pointer, with a Boone and Crockett score of 265 3/8 non-typical, now reigns as Saskatchewan's biggest non-typical. In studying the royal

Photo by Ron Brown

Photo by Ron Brown

Photo by Ron Brown

Photo by Ron Brown

Main Characteristics: Tremendous mass. Circumferences average over 6 6/8". Antlers weigh 11 1/4 pounds.

ELBURN KOHLER, SASKATCHEWAN, 1957

	Right Antler	Left Antler	Difference
Main Beam Length	25 7/8	26 0/8	1/8
1st Point Length	8 3/8	9 4/8	1 1/8
2nd Point Length	14 6/8	11 6/8	3 0/8
3rd Point Length	11 3/8	9 5/8	1 6/8
4th Point Length	7 2/8	7 2/8	–
5th Point Length	–	–	–
1st Circumference	6 6/8	6 5/8	1/8
2nd Circumference	6 5/8	6 5/8	–
3rd Circumference	7 3/8	7 5/8	2/8
4th Circumference	6 5/8	6 2/8	3/8
Total	**95 0/8**	**91 2/8**	**6 6/8**

MISCELLANEOUS STATS	
No. Of Points–Right	16
No. Of Points–Left	17
Total No. Of Points	33
Length Of Abnormals	67 4/8
Greatest Spread	28 4/8
Tip To Tip Spread	10 1/8
Inside Spread	18 3/8

FINAL TALLY	
Inside Spread	18 3/8
Right Antler	95 0/8
Left Antler	91 2/8
Gross Score	204 5/8
Difference	-6 6/8
Subtotal	197 7/8
Abnormals	+67 4/8
NET NON-TYPICAL SCORE	265 3/8

configuration of this buck, which now ranks No. 12 all-time, it is easy to understand why many deer hunters call him "The King of White-Tailed Bucks."

The antlers alone weigh an incredible 11 1/4 pounds. By comparison, the massive Jordan rack only weighs 10 1/4 pounds. The Kohler Buck's antler circumferences average almost seven inches, with 54 4/8 total inches. The antlers consist of 67 4/8 inches of abnormal points. The deep, rich brown color of the antlers

(they've never artificially colored) make the rack a grand masterpiece of nature.

The exact details of how Elburn Kohler shot this massive buck may never be known since he died in 1961. But, we do know that he bagged this buck in the northern coniferous forest somewhere in the vicinity of the small village of White Fox (population 264), located near Tobin Lake in northeastern Saskatchewan. There, Kohler met up with this legendary buck in a true wilderness setting, where most travel was done via float planes and where, even today, whitetail densities remained quite low. Where it was shot was described as "the last road to wilderness."

The year of this noble buck's demise, 1957, was a fascinating year in the history of North American whitetail deer hunting. Eight other whitetails also entered the Saskatchewan record book in '57. That year also saw the widespread distribution of The Wildlife Management Institute's classic deer book, *The Deer of North America*, edited by Walter P. Taylor.

The Kohler Buck is simply awesome, combining incredible mass and character with rugged beauty. Photo by Dick Idol.

In 1957, the greatest storyteller of deer hunting tales was Edmund Ward Smith (1900-1967). He dazzled the deer hunting fraternity with his humorous adventures of Jeff Coongate, the legendary One-Eyed Poacher of Privilege. On the how-to front, Larry Koller's classic, *Shots at Whitetails*, reigned supreme, as did the deer prints of the young Bob Kuhn.

In 1957, big game hunting historian, Grancel Fitz, published *North American Head Hunting*, in which he rightly argued that "you can travel the world over for trophies, far back of beyond you may go,

but one day you'll come back to follow the track of the white-tailed deer in the snow"—the greatest prize of North American hunting. The Kohler Buck is indeed one of these prizes.

When Kohler died in 1961, his mother passed the antlers on to his half-brother, Colin Bishop, who resided on Vancouver Island. Bishop had the antlers scored in British Columbia, and they appeared in the 1971 Boone and Crockett book with a score of 246 7/8. Then, in 1979, the antlers were rescored by a panel of judges from the Boone and Crockett Club. They ultimately ended up with an impressive final score of 265 3/8 non-typical points.

In 1986, Joe Coombs, a well-known taxidermist from Loraqnger, Louisiana, sculpted a new headform for the mount. Then, Joe Meder to Solon, Iowa, one of the world's premier whitetail taxidermists, remounted the head. Joe Meder's artistic taxidermy gives the Kohler Buck the look of royalty that borders on the artistic imagery of Sir Edwin Landseer's classic painting "The Monarch of the Glen."

A fitting pose for "The King of White-Tailed Bucks."

Chapter Twenty-Two

THE CHARLES LISCHKA BUCK

187 4/8 TYPICAL, SASKATCHEWAN, 1973

Tale Of The Tall-Tined Ten

BY GREG MILLER

Charles Lischka knew that the flock of crows circling above one of his pastures could mean only one thing. The coyotes he'd heard howling last night had been successful in their quest for food. Curious as to what the predators had found, Charles decided to investigate the scene. What he found both surprised and shocked him.

"I came around a piece of bush and saw two big bucks with their antlers locked together," he recalled. "One of the bucks was down and obviously dead. The other one was still standing, but he looked like he was about done for."

As he got closer, Charles could see that the coyotes already had eaten on the fallen buck for several days. All that remained of the dead deer was the neck and head. His antlers, however, still remained firmly locked to those of the surviving buck.

"There was no way that buck was going to survive unless we got him loose from the dead deer," he stated. "So, we took a hacksaw and cut off part of the rack from the dead buck. This freed the deer that was still alive. After resting a bit, he took off

Main Characteristics:
Long serpentine brow
tines.

CHARLES LISCHKA, SASKATCHEWAN, 1973

	Right Antler	Left Antler	Difference
Main Beam Length	25 3/8	25 7/8	4/8
1st Point Length	9 3/8	9 0/8	3/8
2nd Point Length	11 0/8	11 0/8	–
3rd Point Length	11 5/8	13 0/8	1 3/8
4th Point Length	10 2/8	9 2/8	1 0/8
5th Point Length	–	–	–
1st Circumference	5 2/8	5 1/8	1/8
2nd Circumference	4 7/8	4 5/8	2/8
3rd Circumference	5 3/8	4 6/8	5/8
4th Circumference	4 6/8	4 0/8	6/8
Total	**87 7/8**	**86 5/8**	**5 0/8**

MISCELLANEOUS STATS	
No. Of Points–Right	5
No. Of Points–Left	6
Total No. Of Points	11
Length Of Abnormals	1 0/8
Greatest Spread	21 5/8
Tip To Tip Spread	14 5/8
Inside Spread	19 0/8

FINAL TALLY	
Inside Spread	19 0/8
Right Antler	87 7/8
Left Antler	86 5/8
Gross Score	**193 4/8**
Difference	-5 0/8
Subtotal	**188 4/8**
Abnormals	-1 0/8
NET TYPICAL SCORE	**187 4/8**

for a nearby chunk of bush."

Although two bucks with their antlers locked is a rare sight anywhere, Charles Lischka wasn't surprised to find that two really big bucks had been involved in this fight to the death. You see, Charles lives near Steelman, Saskatchewan, which is in the heart of some of the best trophy whitetail turf in Northern America. A number of monster bucks from this area had fallen to Charles' gun over the years. While several of those bucks garnered top honors in local big buck contests, a huge 10-point typical Charles shot during

the 1973 season is the focus of this story.

Actually, the hunt on which that big buck was taken started out rather uneventful. Charles and his son had spent most of the day alternately driving around and pushing selected blocks of cover. Even though they had worked hard, the two men hadn't experienced much success. But some time during mid-afternoon, Charles finally managed to push a huge buck out of a thicket.

"Although my son got a pretty good look at the deer, he wasn't able to get off a shot," Charles remembered. "We chased the buck out of a couple more pieces of bush without getting a shot. Finally, we pushed him into a slightly smaller patch of cover. My son told me to go around to the other end of the thicket and he'd walk through it."

Charles was carrying his favorite hunting rifle on this day, a customized .303 British. He had carried this particular weapon on many hunts over the years, and the gun had accounted for a lot of game.

"I shot a bull moose one time at 447 paces with the .303," he stated. "A buddy of mine was standing right next to me when I made the shot, and he couldn't believe it." Charles went on to say that he had won quite a few shooting contests over the years with the gun. "That rifle fits me perfectly. And, I've shot it so much that I know exactly where to hold at most any reasonable distance."

Charles had barely gotten to his selected spot when he heard brush breaking somewhere in the thicket. Then, a big buck burst out of the bush and started high-tailing it across an open field. The range was 250 yards and rapidly increasing. But, Charles felt confident as he raised his trusty .303 and lined up on the running deer.

"I got off two shots before the buck disappeared in another patch of cover," Charles said. "Although the buck was really moving, I felt that at least one of my shots had connected."

A quick check of the buck's trail showed that one bullet had indeed found its mark. Charles and his son took up the trail of the wounded buck, and it wasn't long before they caught up to the deer.

"He gave us the slip at first. In fact, he continued to give us the slip for quite a while," Charles said. "He kept going from one thick slough to the next, and we weren't able to get a clear shot at him. Finally, he made a wrong move and I was able to get a finishing shot."

The two hunters knew that they had taken an exceptional buck as soon as they walked up to the fallen animal. The inside spread of the antlers was pushing 20-inches, and all 10 tines were extremely long. The beams appeared to be over two feet in length, and the antlers boasted fairly heavy bases. More importantly, however, the rack was very symmetrical. From past experience, Charles knew this could prove to be a big factor in the final score.

A few weeks after season, Charles took the antlers from his buck to a big game awards banquet. There, the buck was officially scored at 187 4/8 typical, securing second place for the entire province for the 1973 hunting season. (Interestingly, the buck that beat out Charles's deer in 1973 was taken by George Chalus. The story of his "legendary whitetail" appears elsewhere in this book).

Charles Lischka still lives in the Steelman area and still chases big whitetails at least a few days each season.

"My family bought me a new rifle a few years back, a 7mm Mag. But, I've never really felt comfortable with that gun," he said. "It just doesn't fit me quite right, so it sits in the corner and collects dust. I went right back to carrying my old .303. With that gun, I know if a big buck steps out of the bush, he's in big trouble."

Who can argue with a man who has had so much success at taking trophy whitetails?

Chapter Twenty-Three

THE LOBSTER CLAW BUCK

217 NON-TYPICAL, ILLINOIS, 1990

The Rack With The Ultimate Drop Tine

BY LES DAVENPORT

On November 14, 1990, Avon, Illinois, residents Brian Hoffman and son Mitchell headed afield to collect willow saplings from a rural slough. Brian used the pliant staves to fashion a unique style of furniture. Tree sap had long since withdrawn below ground, offering ideal harvest conditions for the Lincoln Land cane craftsman.

Clouds threatened rain as father and son cut and bundled willows of various lengths. Fifteen-year-old Mitchell eventually grew bored with the task at hand and wandered off to investigate other areas of the slough. Sun-bleached bones scattered about the perimeter of a nearly dry pond caught the young boy's attention. Closer inspection turned up a giant whitetail rack mired in mud near the pond's nucleus.

Mitchell tugged the huge antlers and skull from its resting place and rejoined his father to share the discovery. Not being a whitetail hunter, Brian briefly admired his son's find and suggested that the foul-smelling remanent of a deer be left in the slough. Mitchell asked to show the unusual antlers to his grandfather, Roger

Main Characteristics: Long 13 7/8" drop tine in shape of lobster claw on right main beam.

LOBSTER CLAW, ILLINOIS, 1990

	Right Antler	Left Antler	Difference
Main Beam Length	29 0/8	27 4/8	1 4/8
1st Point Length	7 0/8	5 5/8	1 3/8
2nd Point Length	11 0/8	12 2/8	1 2/8
3rd Point Length	11 5/8	13 2/8	1 5/8
4th Point Length	7 3/8	7 5/8	2/8
5th Point Length	–	–	–
1st Circumference	5 4/8	5 4/8	–
2nd Circumference	4 6/8	5 0/8	2/8
3rd Circumference	4 1/8	4 3/8	2/8
4th Circumference	4 2/8	4 2/8	–
Total	84 5/8	85 3/8	6 4/8

MISCELLANEOUS STATS	
No. Of Points–Right	10
No. Of Points–Left	9
Total No. Of Points	19
Length Of Abnormals	34 0/8
Greatest Spread	22 1/8
Tip To Tip Spread	7 3/8
Inside Spread	19 4/8

FINAL TALLY	
Inside Spread	19 4/8
Right Antler	84 5/8
Left Antler	85 3/8
Gross Score	**189 4/8**
Difference	-6 4/8
Subtotal	183 0/8
Abnormals	+34 0/8
NET NON-TYPICAL SCORE	**217 0/8**

Schieferdecker of Galesburg. Brian agreed to haul the rack home.

Rumors of the antlers spread across Fulton County like fire in a July wheat field. A 15-inch forked drop tine descending from the right main beam inspired considerable commentary. Once marvel over the bizarre claw-like non-typical point ebbed, attention generally focused on the massive 5x5 frame. A forked G-1 and G-2 and five sticker points enhanced the 19-point rack's multidimensional appearance.

At least two local deer hunters identi-fied the drop-tine buck as one they had seen during the 1989 deer season. Oddly, sightings of this unmistakable whitetail occurred almost five miles from the wil-low slough. Neither hunter had knowl-edge of the big deer being wounded, and both men had wondered where the buck relocated.

Two assumptions about its fate might explain puzzling disappearances of other world-class whitetails. First, it is not pre-sumptuous that the Lobster Claw Buck trekked two core areas five miles apart. In 32 years of deer hunting, I have come across a dozen or more cases which corroborate this possibility. One, for example, involved a drop-tine buck hit by a car on a Fulton County road near Farmington. The 201-inch Boone and Crockett non-typical had been spotted several times during twilight crossing expanses of agricultural ground between two sections of timber-

Mitchell Hoffman, who discovered the Lobster Claw Buck, holds his prize. Photo courtesy the Hoffman family.

land separated by several miles. A similar scenario occurred in my home county of Woodford.

Male whitetails that gain enough age to grow world-class antlers rarely prevail over subordinates for more than three years (normally from age four through six). Dominant cornbelt bucks are more likely to claim a dual range during this period of life. If one area becomes pressured, it will be visited only after sundown. When hunter coercion occurs at both ranges, a dominant buck wisely spends daylight hours in isolated outcroppings between domains.

Upon surrendering reign, dominant bucks favor living out their remaining days on a portion of their arena where the activity of humans is nil. Nocturnal demeanor for time-worn bucks helps them avoid conflicts. They die as recluses, their flesh consumed by carnivores and their bones and antlers gnawed away

by calcium-craving rodents.

Secondly, the Lobster Claw's time of demise seems to have correlated with Illinois' firearm deer season, which raises the distinct possibility that this deer was mortally wounded before escaping its pursuer. The fact that expiration befell the animal in a shallow pond raises further speculation about an intestinal hit. Digestive acids leaching through the gut cavity induce a burning sensation soothed by snow, cold water or cool mud. The end result of such an injury, though, is slow and certain death.

If pushed, mature bucks are known to travel great distances subsequent to an intestine wound. Sparse external bleeding makes tracking tough. The distressed deer eventually will seek water to relieve injury and thirst. If not bothered, the lion's share of gut-hit deer die where they first attempt to abate pain. Rivers, lakes and sloughs surely claim many great whitetails that deserved better than an "iffy" shot.

The Lobster Claw Buck may have escaped the pages of this publication and the appreciation of thousands of sportsmen throughout the country had it not been for a curious teenager. Thank you, Mitchell Hoffman.

Chapter Twenty-Four

THE DAVID MANDERSCHEID BUCK

256 7/8 NON-TYPICAL, IOWA, 1977

Brothers Team Up On A Family Legacy

BY BILL WINKE

If things had gone according to schedule, David Manderscheid would have been at the hospital excitedly waiting for his wife to deliver their son, Nathan, instead of hunting deer. Obligingly, Nathan entered the world a week early, allowing David and brother John to spend the weekend hunting near their Jackson County, Iowa, homes. On December 12, 1977, David Manderscheid took one of the largest non-typical bucks of all time, scoring 256 7/8 Boone and Crockett points.

"We were lucky to be hunting there in the first place," said John Manderscheid, David's brother. "David had a group that he usually hunted with, and I hunted with another group. At the last minute that year, we decided to hunt by ourselves in another area. The first weekend of the season, we hunted near Andrew. I took a nice 8-pointer, my first deer, shortly after we got started. The following weekend, we chose an area northwest of Fulton near the farm owned by David's in-laws." (Party hunting is legal in Iowa, making it possible for John to continue hunting.)

As it nears the Mississippi outside of Fulton, the North Fork of the Maquoketa River creates a wide drainage with steep, rugged bluffs. Broad, deep ravines caused by centuries of runoff cut into the slopes as they fall away to the rich bottom land below. It was through this broken country that David and John stalked.

Main Characteristics: 35 scorable points. 23 abnormals add an impressive 73 1/8" to the score.

David Manderscheid, Iowa, 1977

	Right Antler	Left Antler	Difference
Main Beam Length	28 3/8	27 6/8	5/8
1st Point Length	8 5/8	8 0/8	5/8
2nd Point Length	11 2/8	12 6/8	1 4/8
3rd Point Length	10 7/8	9 6/8	1 1/8
4th Point Length	4 7/8	2 4/8	2 3/8
5th Point Length	2 5/8	4 0/8	1 3/8
1st Circumference	5 1/8	5 4/8	3/8
2nd Circumference	4 4/8	4 4/8	–
3rd Circumference	5 4/8	4 6/8	6/8
4th Circumference	5 1/8	5 3/8	2/8
Total	**86 7/8**	**84 7/8**	**9 0/8**

Miscellaneous Stats		Final Tally	
No. Of Points–Right	18	Inside Spread	21 0/8
No. Of Points–Left	17	Right Antler	86 7/8
Total No. Of Points	35	Left Antler	84 7/8
Length Of Abnormals	73 1/8	Gross Score	192 6/8
Greatest Spread	25 2/8	Difference	-9 0/8
Tip To Tip Spread	10 3/8	Subtotal	183 6/8
Inside Spread	21 0/8	Abnormals	+73 1/8
		Net Non- Typical Score	256 7/8

"After working along a hillside for a couple of hours, we met about 10 in the morning near a small grove of pines to take a short break," said John. "The grove was out by itself, but we could see from the light snow on the ground that deer had been going in and out of it.

"We rested a few minutes, then I told Dave to wait there and I would go around the grove and walk back through it toward him. Dave took cover next to a big downed tree. It was really thick in the trees. I would walk and stop, and each time I stopped, I would see the legs of several deer walking in front of me. One time, a buck went across a small opening and I glimpsed a big rack. The deer were all walking directly toward Dave, so I just kept going slow and easy.

"I was near the end of the grove when I heard the deer break out, followed by a shot...then another. Dave was an excellent shot with a slug gun. In fact, he had taken five deer with five slugs, so I figured he had gotten him. When I reached the open, I couldn't see my brother, so I began following the trail and found a few drops of blood and then a few more. Finally, I saw Dave's tracks in the snow alongside the thin blood trail.

"That's when I looked up and saw him walking toward me. He had kind of a shocked look of his face. I knew something was up. I asked him how big the buck was, and Dave said, 'He's about a 4-pointer.' I knew better because I had glimpsed a big rack earlier. We then went back to where the buck lay. His rack was huge.

"Dave said his first shot had only grazed the buck as it ran straight toward him on the trail. As it turned broadside to go past him, he shot again and hit the buck perfectly in the chest, knocking it off balance…and over a 50 to 70-foot bluff!

"We were both concerned that the fall had crushed the huge rack, but it wasn't damaged at all. We had to go to the farmer and borrow a tractor to get the buck out of there. He dressed about 180 pounds."

After the buck had been shown around, the brothers brought him to the local sports shop where proprietor Francis Johnson called game biologist Bob Sheets. Bob rough scored the rack and estimated his age at only three or four years! After the prescribed drying period, the rack was sent to Des Moines to be officially scored. To this day, it

Dave Manderscheid (left) is obviously pleased with his huge non-typical. Photo courtesy the Manderscheid family.

ranks as the second largest non-typical ever killed in Iowa.

The antlers possess a net typical frame scoring 183 6/8 as a 6x6. An additional 73 1/8 points come from 23 scorable abnormals! The buck has 18 points of one inch or more on his right antler and 17 on his left, giving him 35 scorable points in total!

The buck has relatively long main beams, measuring 28 3/8 and 27 6/8 inches, and good mass, with all circumference measurements 4 4/8 inches or better. The G-2s are the longest points, measuring 11 2/8 and 12 6/8 inches. With a 21-inch inside spread, the handsome rack has a tall, elegant appearance.

One of the most unusual features of the Manderscheid Buck is the quantity of thin, fragile points, some of which measure less than an inch. These thin points would have been easily broken off had the buck done any amount of rubbing or fighting. Experts who have examined the rack all agree that this was one deer which avoided fighting.

Tragically, in 1991 at age 39, David Manderscheid lost his life in an industrial accident at his place of employment. According to David's widow, Dena Manderscheid, "Taking that buck was one of the proudest moments of his life."

Chapter Twenty-Five

THE EARL McMASTER BUCK

191 5/8 TYPICAL, MONTANA, 1963

*Montana's Ducks
to Bucks Story*

BY DICK IDOL

Geographically, the Flathead Valley, located in Montana's Flathead County, is an anomaly. It is literally a farmland oasis surrounded by millions of acres of mountainous wilderness. Within the Flathead Valley is a small, hilly area known as the "potholes," thusly named for its many small emerald-colored lakes surrounded by dense evergreens. In the 1960s, this area was a hunter's paradise loaded with ducks, geese, elk, bear and whitetails.

Back in 1963, Earl McMaster worked the 12 midnight until 8:00 a.m. shift at the Anaconda Aluminum Plant in Columbia Falls. This gave him plenty of time to hunt when he got off work. Although it was November, ducks were still on some of the unfrozen lakes, so one afternoon, Earl got in a quick duck hunt at the potholes.

Main Characteristics: Handsome 6x6 main frame with exceptional balance.

EARL MCMASTER, MONTANA, 1963

	Right Antler	Left Antler	Difference
Main Beam Length	26 5/8	26 2/8	3/8
1st Point Length	4 6/8	4 6/8	–
2nd Point Length	13 1/8	13 5/8	4/8
3rd Point Length	12 2/8	11 1/8	1 1/8
4th Point Length	9 6/8	9 6/8	–
5th Point Length	4 0/8	4 5/8	5/8
1st Circumference	5 1/8	5 0/8	1/8
2nd Circumference	4 3/8	4 4/8	1/8
3rd Circumference	4 4/8	4 3/8	1/8
4th Circumference	4 3/8	4 5/8	2/8
Total	88 7/8	88 5/8	3 2/8

MISCELLANEOUS STATS

No. Of Points–Right	6
No. Of Points–Left	7
Total No. Of Points	13
Length Of Abnormals	1 5/8
Greatest Spread	21 5/8
Tip To Tip Spread	13 2/8
Inside Spread	19 0/8

FINAL TALLY

Inside Spread	19 0/8
Right Antler	88 7/8
Left Antler	88 5/8
Gross Score	196 4/8
Difference	-3 2/8
Subtotal	193 2/8
Abnormals	-1 5/8
NET TYPICAL SCORE	191 5/8

When he stopped by the North Fork Bar to have a beer and to visit with Burnie Kuschner, the local deer expert and bar owner, Earl's thoughts weren't on the ducks he'd shot that afternoon; but rather, all he talked about was the many huge deer tracks he'd seen in the fresh snow around the lakes. From the number of running tracks, he knew that rutting activity was well underway and that the bucks were hot after the does.

The next morning, he went back to the same area with his rifle. After a little looking around, he soon shot a big buck chasing a doe. As it turned out, the huge 6x7 scored an incredible 191 5/8 as a typical, placing it among Montana's best.

Interestingly, George Woldstad shot a giant 241 7/8 non-typical in 1960 from the same area. Flathead County still has the distinction of produc-

"From the number of running tracks, he knew that rutting activity was well underway and that the bucks were hot after the does."

"While an inside spread of 19 inches, main beams of just over 26 inches and mass totalling 18 3/8 inches per side make for most respectable numbers, the buck's real strength lies in the number of lengthy tines he possesses."

ing more B&C heads than any other county in Montana.

The McMaster Buck scores as a classic 6x6. While an inside spread of 19 inches, main beams of just over 26 inches and mass totalling 18 3/8 inches per side make for most respectable numbers, the buck's real strength lies in the number of lengthy tines he possesses. Both his G-2s are over 13 inches; his G-3s measure to a net credit of 11 1/8 inches per side; and his G-4s are both a very strong 9 6/8 inches. His bonus G-5s add another 8 inches to his net score. Remarkably, he loses only 3 2/8 inches for side-to-side differences and 1 5/8 inches for his single abnormal.

Obviously, Earl McMaster made a very wise decision shifting from ducks to bucks on that November morning back in 1963.

Chapter Twenty-Six

THE BOB MILLER BUCK

194 2/8 TYPICAL, IOWA, 1977

Archery's No. 5 In The World

BY DICK IDOL

Iowa is now certainly regarded as one of the elite big buck states, but that's a relatively new phenomenon. Prior to 1970, this cornbelt state didn't even have a deer season. Since that time, Iowa's deer hunting has followed a predictable path that has been highly conducive to trophy production, as is normally the case in places with expanding herds.

Typically, an emerging population is extremely healthy because buck/doe ratios are good, the deer density is low, providing plenty of nutritious feed, disease is minimal and, perhaps most importantly, the breeding ritual works the way nature intended. By that, I mean that the biggest bucks do most of the breeding, thus passing along the most superior genes. When the number of deer per square mile is very low, hunting is more difficult; consequently, hunting pressure is minimal. These conditions are ideal for the growth of really big bucks.

When deer numbers increase, hunting pressure starts to build. This hunting pres-

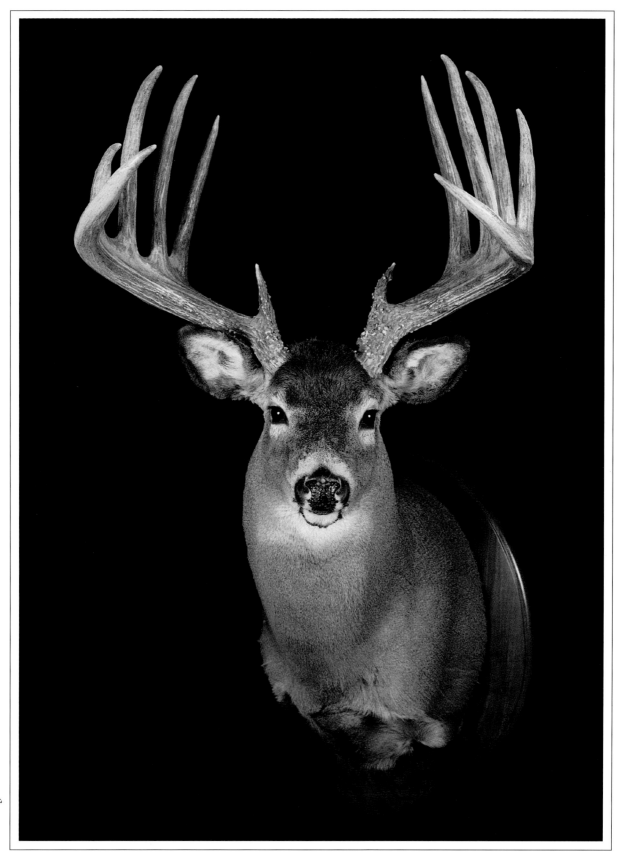

Main Characteristics: Classic 6x6 with short brow tines. Massive main frame.

Bob Miller, Iowa, 1977

	Right Antler	Left Antler	Difference
Main Beam Length	26 5/8	25 0/8	1 5/8
1st Point Length	3 5/8	3 2/8	3/8
2nd Point Length	10 4/8	11 7/8	1 3/8
3rd Point Length	11 5/8	10 7/8	6/8
4th Point Length	10 7/8	8 7/8	2 0/8
5th Point Length	5 2/8	6 4/8	1 2/8
1st Circumference	4 6/8	5 0/8	2/8
2nd Circumference	5 0/8	5 1/8	1/8
3rd Circumference	8 0/8	7 0/8	1 0/8
4th Circumference	6 1/8	6 7/8	6/8
Total	**92 3/8**	**90 3/8**	**9 4/8**

MISCELLANEOUS STATS	
No. Of Points–Right	6
No. Of Points–Left	6
Total No. Of Points	12
Length Of Abnormals	–
Greatest Spread	23 2/8
Tip To Tip Spread	13 1/8
Inside Spread	21 0/8

FINAL TALLY	
Inside Spread	21 0/8
Right Antler	92 3/8
Left Antler	90 3/8
Gross Score	**203 6/8**
Difference	-9 4/8
Subtotal	194 2/8
Abnormals	–
NET TYPICAL SCORE	**194 2/8**

sure is usually heavily weighted toward bucks, and soon, does considerably outnumber the bucks in the herd. As this trend continues, the increased number of does produces a high number of offspring. Before long, the deer density may approach or exceed carrying capacity, decreasing the quality of feed. Of course, as the deer numbers increase, so do the number of hunters. In time, the relative number of mature bucks becomes smaller and smaller as hunters flock to the "popular" spots.

Iowa's super abundant supply of highly nutritious feed, relatively restrictive hunting regulations and fantastic genetics have helped to maintain extraordinary trophy production even as its deer herd has matured. Still, when Bob Miller of Wyoming, Iowa, took to the field in 1977, he was hunting a deer herd very much in the prime stage of this big buck cycle.

Deer had been stocked in several of the upper Midwest states during the 1950s and 1960s, and seasons had remained closed until the early 1970s. When they did open, those states offered some of the best big buck hunting this country has ever known. Throughout the 1970s, dozens of typical and non-typical world-class bucks were taken there.

Bob had been bowhunting for quite a few years and had taken several bucks, though nothing bigger than a medium 8-pointer. During the first five weeks of the 1977 bow season, he had invested approximately 115 hours in hunting from various stands. He had seen some good bucks but nothing spectacular.

It so happened that in early November a few friends came up from southern Missouri to hunt pheasants. During the course of the hunt, the dogs jumped a huge buck. All the hunters, including Bob, stared wide-eyed as the giant whitetail disappeared across a field. The buck was so spectacular that Bob decided to make all out effort to get him with his bow.

Some logging had been done in the area where he suspected the buck was living and had created an upturned willow stump well suited for a ground stand, which Bob generally prefers. Around 3:00 p.m. on November 17, in the heart of the rut, Bob climbed into the clump of willow roots. He had been in the stand only 15 minutes when he saw the huge buck coming down a trail that would bring him within easy bow range. For a change, Murphy's law didn't prevail and Bob got off a good shot. The buck bolted. Bob was sure he'd hit the buck, but he wasn't sure how well.

He could not find the arrow but did manage to find some blood. At least, he knew the buck was hit so he decided to give him a couple of hours, hoping the buck would lay down and die.

When he finally took up the trail, tracking was tough and slow because there was only the occasional fleck of blood. Running tracks and hoof prints provided the primary clues for keeping on the trail.

After considerable twisting and winding through the timber, the buck's trail led into a huge 300-acre standing corn field. The game just moved to a new level of challenge! At that point, Bob decided to leave the buck alone and take up the task the next day.

The next morning, Bob and his buddies were on the trail early. After several hours on hands and knees, they eventually found the deer. He had reached a waterway, where he died with the arrow still in him. He had been hit in the lower spine, probably cutting the dorsal aorta, which accounted for the sparse blood trail and the long distance the buck traveled.

Even though he was very gaunt from heavy rut activity, the buck still dressed 197 pounds. But, his rack was huge, and amazingly symmetrical and clean, totally absent of any abnormal points! His net score turned out to be a whopping 194 2/8 typical, ranking it No. 5 in the world for archery kills. The buck still is the No. 3 typical for the state of Iowa. His mass and symmetry are perhaps the most unique characteristics of this great typical.

After Bob killed his buck, he said he saw five more that season "as big or bigger than the one I shot." Oh, to have hunted Iowa in its heyday...after all, even today, Iowa is as good as it gets anywhere in the world for giant bucks. Just check the records!

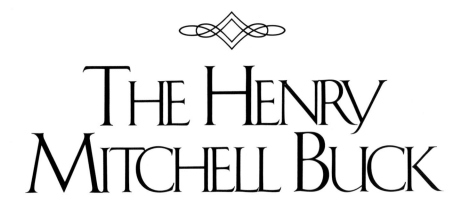

Chapter Twenty-Seven

THE HENRY MITCHELL BUCK

233 2/8 NON-TYPICAL, INDIANA, 1972

A Whopper "Typical" Non-Typical

BY BRAD HERNDON

By the 1970s, rugged Switzerland County, Indiana, had become a place synonymous with trophy whitetails among Hoosiers. And, the county's fame was added to greatly when Henry Mitchell and his brother-in-law, Virgil Ross, went shotgun hunting one November morning in 1972. Here's how it happened.

After driving the 30 miles from Lawrenceburg where he lived, Henry met Virgil at a farm they frequently hunted in Switzerland County. Entering a small hollow, they elected to split up and still-hunt down separate sides of the gully. They had barely parted when Virgil heard a noise. Looking up, he saw the largest whitetail he had ever seen coming over the hill. In the following seconds, both Virgil and Henry fired

Photo by Ron Brown

Henry Mitchell, Indiana, 1972

	Right Antler	Left Antler	Difference
Main Beam Length	27 2/8	25 5/8	1 5/8
1st Point Length	7 2/8	6 1/8	1 1/8
2nd Point Length	13 7/8	13 7/8	–
3rd Point Length	10 6/8	11 3/8	5/8
4th Point Length	10 6/8	10 4/8	2/8
5th Point Length	8 3/8	7 7/8	4/8
6th Point Length	–	4 0/8	4 0/8
1st Circumference	4 7/8	4 7/8	–
2nd Circumference	4 1/8	4 0/8	1/8
3rd Circumference	4 7/8	4 0/8	7/8
4th Circumference	4 5/8	4 4/8	1/8
Total	**96 6/8**	**96 6/8**	**9 2/8**

Main Characteristics: Long-tined, box-shaped non-typical. Gross typical score of 212 2/8.

Miscellaneous Stats	
No. Of Points–Right	9
No. Of Points–Left	11
Total No. Of Points	20
Length Of Abnormals	30 2/8
Greatest Spread	23 0/8
Tip To Tip Spread	7 2/8
Inside Spread	18 6/8

Final Tally	
Inside Spread	18 6/8
Right Antler	96 6/8
Left Antler	96 6/8
Gross Score	**212 2/8**
Difference	-9 2/8
Subtotal	203 0/8
Abnormals	+30 2/8
Net Non-Typical Score	**233 2/8**

several shots at the incredible buck. History credits Henry with making the killing shot.

Looking at the downed whitetail, Henry and Virgil knew it was a big buck—241 pounds field-dressed, in fact. But as with many of history's greatest whitetails, the true magnitude of the deer's rack was not realized for several days. Once it was measured, however, the 20-point, 233 2/8-inch buck became the highest scoring non-typical deer ever taken in Indiana!

Interestingly, Henry's big non-typical also had a world-class basic typical frame, grossing an impressive 212 2/8 inches and netting 203 as a 6x7. Extremely tall tines, an 18 6/8 inside spread and upward sweeping main beam tips make the rack one of great beauty.

While Henry ended up with his name on a state record whitetail, his reign was short-lived. In 1977, Zolton Dobsa of Cincinnati, Ohio, ventured to, you guessed it, Switzerland County to shotgun hunt for deer. He returned home with a giant non-typical scoring an amazing 254 1/8 points, making it a new state record that still stands today.

Henry Mitchell, a real sportsman, passed away in 1989. It was said of Henry, who was a union painter by voca-

Henry Mitchell and his 233 2/8 non-typical, which has a 212 2/8-point gross typical frame. Photo courtesy the Mitchell family.

tion, that he made a point to "get laid off right before every deer season." He hunted and fished for about everything there was to pursue in Indiana, plus he hunted bear in many parts of the United States and Canada. But, Henry left behind more than the antlers and story of his great buck; he also left behind the influences he had on other people. One case in point should be shared here.

Henry was a man who was willing to take the time to be a teacher of young people. In the winter, he spent much of his time doing taxidermy work. He often allowed teenage boys to come into his taxidermy shop, where he gladly showed them the techniques employed in mounting a deer. Two of the boys he taught, Jay McAdams and Terry Storey, now do taxidermy work themselves. As one might expect, along the way Henry also did more than a little teaching about hunting.

Terry picked up a lot about deer hunting from Henry. And, it somehow seems appropriate that in 1988, a year before Henry's death, Terry tagged a typical buck in Dearborn County that netted 189 3/8, one of the best typical whitetails ever taken in the state. Henry must have been proud!

Chapter Twenty-Eight

THE HOMER PEARSON BUCK

233 7/8 Non-Typical, Wisconsin, 1937

Husband/Wife Team Bring Home An Instant Legend

By Rob Wegner

I n 1937, a very significant year in the history of Wisconsin deer hunting, Aldo Leopold, the chairman of the newly founded Department of Wildlife Management at the University of Wisconsin—Madison, issued a warning of an impending whitetail deer eruption. Leopold's friend, Gordon MacQuarrie, who had just become the outdoor editor of the *Milwaukee Journal,* echoed his concerns of an exploding deer herd.

Also in 1937, the Wisconsin Conservation Department conducted deer drives throughout the state and estimated the deer population at 28.6 animals per section. A buck-only season each even-numbered year had prevailed since 1924. In 1937, the Conservation Commission recommended the beginning of a more liberal deer harvest. As a result, the 1937 Wisconsin deer hunt was the first consecutive deer hunting season since 1923 and 1924.

That season witnessed the first emergence of "Save the Deer" clubs and stringent public criticism of deer management policies. The season lasted for three days,

Main Characteristics: Famous Wisconsin deer shot in 1937. Very wide outside spread of 30 1/8". 31 total points.

HOMER PEARSON, WISCONSIN, 1937

	Right Antler	Left Antler	Difference
Main Beam Length	27 0/8	26 7/8	1/8
1st Point Length	7 4/8	6 6/8	6/8
2nd Point Length	11 3/8	10 7/8	4/8
3rd Point Length	9 0/8	9 0/8	–
4th Point Length	5 6/8	6 5/8	7/8
5th Point Length	1 3/8	2 2/8	7/8
1st Circumference	5 5/8	5 3/8	2/8
2nd Circumference	5 6/8	5 7/8	1/8
3rd Circumference	6 2/8	6 4/8	2/8
4th Circumference	5 1/8	5 5/8	4/8
Total	**84 6/8**	**85 6/8**	**4 2/8**

MISCELLANEOUS STATS	
No. Of Points–Right	16
No. Of Points–Left	15
Total No. Of Points	31
Length Of Abnormals	46 1/8
Greatest Spread	30 1/8
Tip To Tip Spread	15 2/8
Inside Spread	21 4/8

FINAL TALLY	
Inside Spread	21 4/8
Right Antler	84 6/8
Left Antler	85 6/8
Gross Score	192 0/8
Difference	-4 2/8
Subtotal	187 6/8
Abnormals	+46 1/8
NET NON-TYPICAL SCORE	233 7/8

November 26-28, with a bag limit of one forked-horn buck. A deer license cost one dollar. The records say that 90,906 hunters participated in the hunt, resulting in an estimated kill of 14,835 whitetails, which represented a 16 percent success rate.

In 1937, Mr. And Mrs. Homer Pearson teamed up to take this buck and soon found themselves the focus of tremendous attention from sportsmen and the media. Photo courtesy the Pearson family.

At the end of the 1930s, historian Otis Bersing reported in his *A Century of Wisconsin Deer,* "more than two times as many bucks were taken (that year) as were bagged during any deer season of the 1920s."

Two of the most successful deer hunters in historical 1937 were Mr. and Mrs. Homer Pearson, two Burnett County farmers. On November 28, they teamed up to bag a 31-point buck, scoring 233 7/8 non-typical points. For many years, it was displayed at the Friendly Buckhorn Bar in Rice Lake, Wisconsin.

Unusual weather prevailed during the 1937 season. In Burnett and Polk counties, the first day of the season was extremely foggy and in many places the snow had practically disappeared. The second day of the season brought a general storm throughout Wisconsin, and many deer hunters left the woods, apparently anticipating a heavy snowfall. The third day was clear and cold with a fresh tracking snow. The Pearsons succeeded on that final day when others had given up.

While dragging the buck back to their car, the Pearsons met Chauncey Weitz, one of the most colorful game wardens of the period, who spent more time prowling the back areas of Polk and Burnett counties than any other man. Weitz was so impressed with this unusual non-typical buck that he sent the following report back to the main headquarters in Madison.

"The Pearsons left home before dawn on the morning of November 28 and drove 28 miles to their former home in the township of Lorain in Polk County. From there, they hunted north and east along Sand Creek. Mrs. Pearson had a .22 rifle and she drove the thickets for her husband, who was armed with a .30-30 Winchester carbine which he has owned for 22 years. About 1 o'clock, Mr. Pearson saw a buck deer with big antlers break cover about 100 yards from him. He fired and the deer, struck in the shoulder, fell to the ground. When the hunters reached the deer, Mrs. Pearson fired a shot into its head to quiet its struggles. After this, the deer was dressed and dragged out to the car where it was loaded and taken to the farm home of the hunters, a mile and a half east of Almena.

"Mr. Pearson is a farmer and is very much in favor of the buck law and claims that deer is the only kind of game that he ever hunts.

On display at the "FRIENDLY BUCKHORN"   2775

"WORLD'S RECORD DEER" at Rice Lake, Wisconsin

Advertised as the "world's record deer," the full-body mount of the Pearson Buck was on display at the Friendly Buckhorn Bar in Rice Lake, Wisconsin, for years. Photo courtesy Dick Idol.

cle, the newspaper noted that a steady stream of visitors converged on the farm to examine the fallen monarch. The story of the buck aroused such widespread interest that even the vice-president of the United States, John A.

"The deer was killed just east of Sand Creek in the township of Roosevelt, Burnett County.

"The horn formation on this head is remarkable. The right horn is six and a half inches in circumference at the base; the left, six and a fourth inches. The right horn has 25 points and the left has 18. The points are 16 inches apart in front, and the widest spread is about 30 inches. The longest points are nine inches long, and all points have several smaller points growing out from them.

"The total weight of the buck rough-dressed was 218 pounds, which is an indication that the deer is not exceptionally large."

The immediate response in the newspapers ran a little bit beyond reality. On December 20, 1937, the *Milwaukee Sentinel* ran an article entitled "103 Points in Deer Antlers." In this arti-

"The story of the buck aroused such widespread interest that even the vice-president of the United States, John A. Garner, sent Homer a letter of inquiry, as did hundreds of other people."

Garner, sent Homer a letter of inquiry, as did hundreds of other people. According to the newspaper report, "many taxidermists offered to mount the head without cost and Pearson received offers up to $200 for the unmounted animal."

The October 1938 issue of the *Wisconsin Sportsman* insisted that "this buck, an old patriarch, had a head of antlers with over a hundred points!" Even a special representative from the State Historical Society also claimed the buck had 103 points.

A correspondent for the *Milwaukee Journal* wrote as follows: "A freak set of deer horns with 50 points was taken during the deer season by Homer Pearson of Almena. He shot the buck in the woods north of Cumberland. The antlers have an unusual spread. Such freak heads are only occasionally reported."

The December/January 1937/38 issue of the *Wisconsin Conservation Bulletin* simply stated that the Pearsons bagged "the best hat rack that came out of the Wisconsin woods during the 1937 season."

The Pearsons were obviously pleased with their legendary buck, but they were less pleased with the new deer management policies calling for drastic reductions in the deer herd, which provoked a storm of protest. A half century of Wisconsin deer hunting would have to pass before "buck-only hunters," such as the Pearsons, would understand the dire need to harvest antlerless deer as deer populations increase.

In his 1937 report

> *"A half century of Wisconsin deer hunting would have to pass before 'buck-only hunters,' such as the Pearsons, would understand the dire need to harvest antlerless deer as deer populations increase."*

published in the *Wisconsin Conservation Bulletin,* Deputy Director Ernie Swift noted that "the 1937 deer season is over and with its completion come the various reactions of hunters and non-hunters. I marvel at times at the opinions which are expressed on the deer question by those who go into the woods no oftener than once a year. In many instances, the reaction of the hunter is based on whether he succeeded in bagging his buck. If unsuccessful and a poor sport, either the law or the season is wrong or there are no deer; if successful, everything is as it should be."

With their 233 7/8-inch non-typical, the Pearsons certainly had every reason to feel that "everything is as it should be."

Chapter Twenty-Nine

THE KENT PETRY BUCK

199 2/8 TYPICAL, MONTANA, 1966

One Of The "Classiest" All-Time Typicals

BY DICK IDOL

Western Montana is a largely untamed land of towering mountains and fertile valleys, of deep snow and vast tracts of evergreen forests. It is also home to perhaps the widest variety of big game animals in the Lower 48. Among its more notable inhabitants are elk, moose, mule deer, bighorn sheep, Rocky Mountain goats, black bears, grizzlies, cougars, wolves and even a sprinkling of Far North species like lynx and wolverine. Oh, yeah...western Montana is also home to whitetails—some very big whitetails.

It was in this wilderness setting one cold morning in late November, 1966, that Kent Petry parked his Jeep along an old, snow-covered logging road in Flathead County, Montana, and climbed out, soon to write his name among the legends of whitetail hunting. With the wind in his face, he eased a mile or so up the road, watching for deer. Then, at around 9 a.m., he decided to sit for a few minutes on a stump. The rut was at its peak now, and the deep snow revealed plenty of deer sign.

As Kent scanned the woods, he spotted two does and a huge buck moving behind

KENT PETRY, MONTANA, 1966

	Right Antler	Left Antler	Difference
Main Beam Length	27 0/8	27 1/8	1/8
1st Point Length	6 3/8	6 3/8	–
2nd Point Length	15 1/8	13 7/8	1 2/8
3rd Point Length	13 6/8	13 5/8	1/8
4th Point Length	9 3/8	11 6/8	2 3/8
5th Point Length	–	–	–
1st Circumference	5 2/8	5 0/8	2/8
2nd Circumference	4 4/8	4 3/8	1/8
3rd Circumference	4 6/8	4 7/8	1/8
4th Circumference	4 4/8	4 5/8	1/8
Total	**90 5/8**	**91 5/8**	**4 4/8**

Main Characteristics: A buck of beauty and balance. Upturned main beams give striking appearance.

MISCELLANEOUS STATS

No. Of Points–Right	5
No. Of Points–Left	5
Total No. Of Points	10
Length Of Abnormals	–
Greatest Spread	24 3/8
Tip To Tip Spread	18 7/8
Inside Spread	21 4/8

FINAL TALLY

Inside Spread	21 4/8
Right Antler	90 5/8
Left Antler	91 5/8
Gross Score	**203 6/8**
Difference	-4 4/8
Subtotal	**199 2/8**
Abnormals	–
NET TYPICAL SCORE	**199 2/8**

some thick spruces. When the monster walked out, he jerked his head up and stared at Kent, who had his .30/06 Remington ready. But, Kent was not prepared for what now stood before him.

"I'll never forget that magnificent sight," the hunter remembered. "His frosty breath looked like smoke around his head, and those antlers looked three feet tall."

Despite being rattled at the sight of the huge antlers, Kent's aim was true and one of the best 10-pointers in history went down.

Years passed before the buck came to the attention of the whitetail world. A co-worker coaxed Kent into having the huge typical officially measured. He was scored at 199 2/8 net Boone and Crockett points, enough to rank No. 2 in Montana. Even then, Kent never entered him, but word got out about

> *"I'll never forget that magnificent sight," the hunter remembered. "His frosty breath looked like smoke around his head, and those antlers looked three feet tall."*

> *"Numbers alone don't adequately describe this buck; his classic confirmation is the real key to his majestic appearance. The upturned main beams serve to enhance the buck's appearance and make him look even larger."*

the buck and he was soon "discovered," eventually ending up featured on the pages of *North American WHITETAIL* magazine.

Many whitetail connoisseurs consider this one of the greatest and most attractive 10-pointers ever. A clean 5x5 with no non-typical points and only 4 4/8 inches of side-to-side deductions, this buck is remarkably symmetrical. Everything about him is good—long 27-inch main beams, 19 inches of mass per beam, four tines over 13 4/8 inches (five over 11 4/8) and a 21 4/8-inch inside spread. But, numbers alone don't adequately describe this buck; his classic confirmation is the real key to his majestic appearance. The upturned main beams serve to enhance the buck's appearance and make him look even larger. Great size and beauty—a winning combination in the mind of any trophy whitetail hunter.

Chapter Thirty

THE
JAMES RATH BUCK

231 2/8 NON-TYPICAL, MINNESOTA, 1977

The Very Embodiment
Of North Country Giants

BY DICK IDOL

As the summer of 1977 rolled along, a buck on a farm in Renville County, Minnesota, was growing an incredible set of antlers. Between haying and other farm operations, members of the Rath family frequently saw him foraging on the nutritious crops, his massive, velvet-covered headgear becoming larger each day.

Jim Rath had grown up on this 350-acre farm near Winthrop, and he'd seen several huge bucks over the years. But, none was as spectacular as this one. With only a spike buck to his credit, Jim wasn't an experienced trophy hunter. Still, he knew he had to give this monster non-typical a sincere effort during the upcoming gun season.

The countryside in this area consists primary of farmland with scattered pockets of trees and brush, ideally suited to producing bucks of magnum caliber. Jim, his dad, his brothers and an occasional friend often hunted together on the farm, making short drives or using other methods as the situation dictated. During the summer and fall, Jim's dad had noted that the local monster buck favored a relatively narrow grove of trees about 300 yards long. Other good groves nearby couldn't be over-

Main Characteristics: Magnificent non-typical with good mass and classic appearance.

JAMES RATH, MINNESOTA, 1977

	Right Antler	Left Antler	Difference
Main Beam Length	26 1/8	30 1/8	4 0/8
1st Point Length	7 2/8	8 1/8	7/8
2nd Point Length	12 1/8	13 6/8	1 5/8
3rd Point Length	12 0/8	12 4/8	4/8
4th Point Length	8 6/8	9 0/8	2/8
5th Point Length	–	–	–
1st Circumference	5 2/8	5 1/8	1/8
2nd Circumference	5 4/8	5 5/8	1/8
3rd Circumference	6 4/8	7 0/8	4/8
4th Circumference	6 3/8	6 1/8	2/8
Total	89 7/8	97 3/8	8 2/8

MISCELLANEOUS STATS	
No. Of Points–Right	10
No. Of Points–Left	9
Total No. Of Points	19
Length Of Abnormals	31 4/8
Greatest Spread	25 6/8
Tip To Tip Spread	14 1/8
Inside Spread	20 6/8

FINAL TALLY	
Inside Spread	20 6/8
Right Antler	89 7/8
Left Antler	97 3/8
Gross Score	208 0/8
Difference	-8 2/8
Subtotal	199 6/8
Abnormals	+31 4/8
NET NON-TYPICAL SCORE	231 2/8

looked as hideouts, but at least, this buck's general range was known.

Finally, the two-day November gun season arrived and the hunt began. The first day was spent making drives here and there around the area, but the mega buck wasn't seen. On the second day, Jim, his dad and a couple of friends made plans to hunt together. They decided to start off by driving the 300-yard-long grove where Jim's dad suspected the high-tined buck lived.

Jim and a friend were posted on the east end as Jim's dad and another friend began the drive on the west end. Jim had a good feeling about his spot, as he visualized the big buck crashing through the trees. He knew a clear shot would be tough to get because the trees were very dense in this grove. He had picked out a 25-foot-wide opening that hopefully would afford a quick shot.

As the drivers made their way through the dense stand, Jim heard his dad yell, "A buck is breaking out to the side!"

Jim looked, but it was only a small buck. Then, he heard a loud crash in the brush. Another animal was headed toward him. As the hunter pointed his slug-loaded Ithaca 12 gauge toward the tiny opening 20 yards away, he caught glimpses of a huge buck. A wall of antlers entered the opening, followed by a huge, dark body, and Jim fired. The heavy slug caught the buck squarely in the neck, causing him to turn a somersault.

As Jim approached, he could hardly contain himself. He knew this was the largest rack he'd ever seen. The hunters field-dressed the animal and took the rack to a local sporting goods store, where it won the deer contest hands down. The buck's field-dressed weight was an impressive 265 pounds.

Upon examination of the jawbone, game department officials estimated that this incredible buck was only 3 1/2 years old when shot. Even though at first this seems impossible, it could be true. Jim's dad never had seen the buck before the summer of 1977, indicating he probably had been a 2 1/2-

From the side, the Rath Buck literally has a wall of tines. Photo by Dick Idol.

This massive non-typical, which was estimated to be only 3 1/2 years of age, has a very symmetrical appearance. Photo by Dick Idol.

year-old the previous season and had carried a rack of more normal size.

If we were to conjure up a dream buck, our imaginations would have to work overtime to visualize a more spectacular trophy. This rack clearly has it all—height, mass, points, spread and, on a more subjective level, beauty. We can only imagine what this deer might have looked like if he'd survived another two or three years!

Certainly, it stands to reason that his rack would have grown even larger if he'd made it into the "prime" of life. Even so, he's still among the most impressive whitetails of all time.

The score doesn't truly reveal how impressive this buck is. For instance, if the Rath Buck hadn't grown any abnormal points (and the majority of 3 1/2-year-old bucks don't), he would have netted 199 6/8 as a clean 5x5, making him a Top 10 typical. On the other hand, I'd say the average buck that scores around 230 non-typical (as this one does) will have close to 60 inches of non-typical points present, as opposed to the 31 4/8 inches this deer actually grew. For sheer appeal to hunters, this Minnesota monster is tough to beat.

Chapter Thirty-One

THE LARRY RAVELING BUCK

282 NON-TYPICAL, IOWA, 1973

Old "Rag Horn" — Former No. 2 And Still Awesome

BY DICK IDOL

Larry Raveling couldn't believe his eyes. As the monster whitetail buck lumbered toward him, he could see a huge rack. But, why were a pair of white drawers impaled on the points? All the startled hunter could think of was how some poor bowhunter or innocent old lady probably had one heck of a story to tell! Actually, Larry couldn't swear that what he saw was somebody's underwear, but it was white cloth of some kind, and it surely looked like a pair of drawers.

As Larry watched the deer coming his way, he was besieged with a severe case of buck fever and promptly sent a shotgun slug clean over the buck's back as he passed. The big non-typical disappeared before Larry could fire another shot, but as luck would have it, a forkhorn followed the big one and Larry made a clean kill on his first buck ever. Old "Rag Horn" escaped the drive and wasn't seen again all season.

This memorable deer drive took place near Petersen, Iowa, in December 1972. Larry was 19 years old, but despite having been raised on a hog farm in prime deer country, he'd never even tried deer hunting before. His appetite now whetted, he

Photo by Ron Brown

Main Characteristics: Tremendous non-typical from Iowa with 96 7/8" of abnormal points. Three drop tines.

LARRY RAVELING, IOWA, 1973

	Right Antler	Left Antler	Difference
Main Beam Length	26 1/8	27 0/8	7/8
1st Point Length	9 0/8	9 5/8	5/8
2nd Point Length	12 2/8	13 6/8	1 4/8
3rd Point Length	9 1/8	9 3/8	2/8
4th Point Length	6 7/8	5 4/8	1 3/8
5th Point Length	1 1/8	–	1 1/8
1st Circumference	6 5/8	6 2/8	3/8
2nd Circumference	4 2/8	4 2/8	–
3rd Circumference	3 7/8	4 0/8	1/8
4th Circumference	4 3/8	4 0/8	3/8
Total	**83 5/8**	**83 6/8**	**6 5/8**

MISCELLANEOUS STATS

No. Of Points–Right	15
No. Of Points–Left	14
Total No. Of Points	29
Length Of Abnormals	96 7/8
Greatest Spread	26 6/8
Tip To Tip Spread	20 0/8
Inside Spread	24 3/8

FINAL TALLY

Inside Spread	24 3/8
Right Antler	83 5/8
Left Antler	83 6/8
Gross Score	191 6/8
Difference	-6 5/8
Subtotal	185 1/8
Abnormals	+96 7/8
NET NON-TYPICAL SCORE	282 0/8

often thought of the big non-typical he'd missed. The next year, he planned to spend more time hunting that area the big buck lived.

Because of the small patches of cover, deer drives work very well in Iowa farm country. Other hunting methods were virtually unheard of in that area back then, partly because the short slug season was quite a social event. Friends and family enjoyed getting together for fun, food and the excitement of the deer drives.

As the 1973 season rolled around, Larry heard talk that another local farmer had been seeing a very large buck in his fields. Sure enough, it was near the area where Larry had missed the monster the year before. Most likely, it was the same buck, and Larry and his cousins would be there opening day.

Finally, the first morning of the December season arrived. After the formalities of breakfast and driving the hogs out from under the trucks, the group was off to an intriguing 20-acre patch of timber just across the road from where Larry had missed the big buck the previous season. Larry was a stander on the first drive, and he was hunkered down beside a tree just below the road. As he heard

Larry Raveling poses with one of the largest bucks ever killed by a known hunter. Photo by Dick Idol.

the drivers in the distance, something rustled the leaves off to one side of him and he promptly heard a shot. A buddy shouted, "I got him!"

As it turned out, he just thought he'd gotten him.

Fortunately, a local bowhunter who knew Larry and his friends was driving past and saw the huge non-typical cross the road after the shot. A closer look at the crossing point did turn up a small amount of blood but not enough to trail the buck. Plans were made to drive the timber patch he'd just entered. Beyond it lay the boundary of a state park, and the buck was heading in that direction. Several standers quickly lined up along the boundary just outside the park, while Larry and the other drivers started in from the front side.

After Larry had traveled a few hundred yards, he topped a little rise that had a draw just beyond it. Across that draw stood a deer with its head behind some bushes. Finally, Larry detected antlers and shot.

As Larry approached the fallen buck, he could see an awesome rack. He bent over, counted 29 antler points and said to himself, "Ain't nobody going to believe this!" The thought actually occurred to him

> *"As Larry approached the fallen buck, he could see an awesome rack. He bent over, counted 29 antler points and said to himself, 'Ain't nobody going to believe this!'"*

that the buck's antlers looked even bigger without the linens than they had with them!

Larry's friends convinced him that his buck was big enough to mount. It was decided that the meat was probably no good, because a "29-year-old buck (one year for each

This is a truck full of buck! Photo courtesy Dick Idol.

point) had to be tough." But, Larry saved the venison anyway, and it turned out to be fairly tasty. Only later did he learn that the number of points on a rack has absolutely nothing to do with the deer's age.

Word eventually spread about the monster non-typical, and it was scored by an official Boone and Crockett measurer. It totaled an unbelievable 282 net points, ranking it as the potential No. 2 trophy in the world at that time. But first, it would have to be verified by a panel of B&C measurers, as is customary for all of the top trophies entered in a given three-year Awards Period. To do this, the head had to be shipped to Denver, where B&C's 1975 judges' panel was to meet.

As Larry recalled, "A trip to Denver was quite an experience for a 'corn-field jockey' like me, who had hardly traveled out of Iowa before."

His first plane trip found him sitting outside the Denver airport with a huge crate too large to go into a cab. So, Larry

had to tear the crate apart right there, give the lumber away and walk through the airport while carrying his mounted buck. Needless to say, he received some strange looks from bystanders.

The Raveling Buck finally made it into the hands of B&C officials, who confirmed him at 282 points and declared him the world's new No. 2 non-typical. Larry and his wife attended the banquet, at which the hunter was presented the top award for non-typical whitetails during that three-year period.

This magnificent rack is definitely among the finest ever, despite the fact that the buck has a major point broken off at the base of the right brow tine. This missing point has a "mate" on the left antler that is almost 10 inches long. Judging from the corresponding size of the bases of those points, it appears reasonable that the broken tine could have been at least 10 inches long, increasing the score to 292 points or more and setting a new world record. (Jeff Benson's 286-point deer from Texas, shot in 1892, was then the No. 1 non-typical.)

The Raveling Buck clearly has impressive overall size and great mass. However, his unique combination of features is what makes him one of the greatest non-typicals of all time. First, he has a very typical look, with five long, matching points on each side. The beams are very heavy, as are the points. Drop tines are common on many of the biggest non-typicals, but are seldom as evenly matched as on this buck. The 26 6/8-inch outside spread of the main beams is also exceptional.

I've decided I want to be a "corn-field jockey,"

"The Raveling Buck clearly has impressive overall size and great mass. However, his unique combination of features is what makes him one of the greatest non-typicals of all time."

too. Anyone who can go from a forkhorn his first year of deer hunting to taking the No. 2 whitetail in the world in his second must know something the rest of us don't. If Larry ever gets a bigger deer than the Rag Horn Buck, I plan to move to Iowa, plant a corn field and buy 100 hogs.

Chapter Thirty-Two

THE CARL RUNYAN BUCK

230 5/8 Non-Typical, Michigan, 1942

*A Legendary Buck
From a Legendary Land*

By Greg Miller

C arl W. Runyan was a deer hunter from Buchanan, Michigan. Buchanan is located in the far southwestern corner of the state. The shores of Lake Michigan lie roughly 25 miles west of Buchanan, while the Indiana border is a mere eight miles south. I bring this bit of geographic information to your attention to point out some of the adversity Carl had to overcome back in 1942 just to get to the area that produced his trophy buck. You see, Carl shot his deer in Iron County, located far to the north in the Michigan's Upper Peninsula (UP), itself a legendary name among deer hunters.

To reach his hunting area, Carl had a couple of choices. He could swing down around the southern tip of Lake Michigan, go through northern Illinois then drive the full length of Wisconsin before crossing into the UP near Iron Mountain, Michigan. Or, he could drive the entire length of lower Michigan, cross the toll bridge that goes between Mackinaw City and St. Ignace then head west and traverse nearly the entire Upper Peninsula to reach Iron County, which is located on the Michigan/Wisconsin border. No matter which way he chose to reach the UP from his

CARL RUNYAN, MICHIGAN, 1942

	Right Antler	Left Antler	Difference
Main Beam Length	25 1/8	26 4/8	1 3/8
1st Point Length	7 0/8	7 1/8	1/8
2nd Point Length	10 6/8	11 4/8	6/8
3rd Point Length	9 2/8	10 3/8	1 1/8
4th Point Length	7 5/8	7 6/8	1/8
5th Point Length	3 6/8	5 2/8	1 4/8
6th Point Length	–	1 5/8	1 5/8
1st Circumference	6 1/8	6 3/8	2/8
2nd Circumference	5 0/8	5 0/8	–
3rd Circumference	4 4/8	4 6/8	2/8
4th Circumference	4 4/8	4 6/8	2/8
Total	83 5/8	91 0/8	7 3/8

Main Characteristics: Exceptionally wide spread of 29 3/8". Inside spread credit in final score is only 26 4/8", since spread exceeds greatest main beam length.

MISCELLANEOUS STATS

No. Of Points–Right	13
No. Of Points–Left	11
Total No. Of Points	24
Length Of Abnormals	36 7/8
Greatest Spread	29 3/8
Tip To Tip Spread	28 6/8
Inside Spread	28 4/8

FINAL TALLY

Inside Spread	26 4/8
Right Antler	83 5/8
Left Antler	91 0/8
Gross Score	201 1/8
Difference	-7 3/8
Subtotal	193 6/8
Abnormals	+36 7/8
NET NON-TYPICAL SCORE	230 5/8

hometown, it was obvious that Carl had quite a drive—back when there were no smooth, four-lane freeways and comfortable, reliable, 4-WD pickups.

Apparently, there were at least three other men from the Buchanan area who, like Carl, were serious deer hunters, for they joined Carl on his trip to the UP for the 1942 deer season. These men, Walt Reese, A.G. Shoeford and Walter H. Reese, must have shared Carl's enthusiasm for the wilderness hunting to be found in Iron County. After much planning and preparation, the four men set out on their long journey.

Upon reaching their selected campsite, they quickly set about the business of getting everything organized for a week's hunt. Surely, the men must have been excited about being able to spend an extended amount of time chasing whitetails in such a wild, unspoiled area. And, I would imagine more than one of them entertained thoughts of downing a huge "swamp buck."

But as it so often goes in this sport, the hunt proved to be filled with more expectation than success. Although the men hunted hard for nearly a full week, they still didn't have any venison to show for their efforts. Then, on the morning of November 18, the last day of their hunt, Carl took his trusty .32 Special and headed out once more. The spot he had selected to hunt lay on the edge of a thick cedar swamp. Walter Reese accompanied Carl into the area, taking up his vigil a short distance away.

Carl Runyan shot this great buck in one of whitetail hunting's legendary places, Michigan's Upper Peninsula. Photo courtesy the Runyan family.

Not long after getting settled, Carl detected movement about 75 yards from his stand. After a bit, he could make out parts of a deer. But with the cover so thick, it took him a while to determine whether or not it was a buck. Then, all of a sudden, he saw part of an antler. Now he knew for sure! Not hesitating, he brought the .32 Special to his shoulder, lined up the sights on the chest cavity of the buck and squeezed off a shot. The soft-point bullet found its mark, and the deer dropped in its tracks.

Carl approached the downed animal, not yet knowing just how big the buck was. However, when he got a little closer, he could see a massive set of antlers sticking far above the snow. At that point, he stopped and just stared. The next thing he knew, Walter was standing next to him. Together, the two men approached the big deer. As they drew closer, Walter began to wonder if maybe Carl hadn't accidentally shot a bull elk. That fear subsided when they finally walked up to the buck. I'm sure there was a bit of back-slapping and handshaking at that point.

Walter helped Carl with field-dressing chores, after which the two men dragged the monster buck back to camp. The next day, the four hunters broke camp and loaded the buck on top of their vehicle. During a breakfast stop in Iron Mountain, Carl met Buck Erickson, the sports editor for a local newspaper called the *Iron Mountain News*. One look at the deer and Buck suggested that Carl should enter his trophy in a contest sponsored by the *Detroit Free Press* newspaper. Carl took his advice and wound up taking two first place awards; one for widest spread and the other for most points.

With 24 scorable points, excellent symmetry, good mass and a remarkable inside spread of 28 4/8 inches, Carl Runyon's 230 5/8-point non-typical remains one of the most impressive deer ever taken in Michigan. He is certainly a buck worthy of his status as a "legendary whitetail."

Chapter Thirty-Three

THE C.W. SHELTON BUCK

185 2/8 TYPICAL, KENTUCKY, 1964

The Legend Of "Big (Wide) Red"

BY DICK IDOL

While most whitetail bucks have achieved legendary status only after death, a few were in that category while still alive. Such is the case with a Kentucky buck known to many whitetail fanatics simply as "Big Red." Even before this giant was killed, many local hunters knew of him, and his legend has only grown in the years since he was taken.

Like many other sportsmen in the Bluegrass State, C.W. Shelton grew up around hunting. However, talk of monster bucks was a relatively new thing in the Elkton area back in 1963 since that area of Kentucky hadn't had legal deer hunting in modern times.

But that year, a buck in the Elkton area was the talk of the town, so to speak, and was indeed well on his way to becoming a legend. According to an account of the hunt printed in a local publication in 1964, "hundreds" of hunters had heard about

C.W. Shelton, Kentucky, 1964

	Right Antler	Left Antler	Difference
Main Beam Length	30 0/8	29 2/8	6/8
1st Point Length	8 2/8	8 7/8	5/8
2nd Point Length	9 5/8	9 2/8	3/8
3rd Point Length	9 7/8	9 2/8	5/8
4th Point Length	8 7/8	6 2/8	2 5/8
5th Point Length	–	–	–
1st Circumference	5 2/8	5 2/8	–
2nd Circumference	4 7/8	4 7/8	–
3rd Circumference	5 3/8	5 3/8	–
4th Circumference	5 5/8	5 2/8	3/8
Total	**87 6/8**	**83 5/8**	**5 3/8**

Main Characteristics: Exceptionally wide outside spread of 34 4/8". Inside spread exceeds longest beam, thus spread credit is only 30".

Miscellaneous Stats

No. Of Points–Right	8
No. Of Points–Left	8
Total No. Of Points	16
Length Of Abnormals	10 6/8
Greatest Spread	34 4/8
Tip To Tip Spread	27 5/8
Inside Spread	30 2/8

Final Tally

Inside Spread	30 0/8
Right Antler	87 6/8
Left Antler	83 5/8
Gross Score	201 3/8
Difference	-5 3/8
Subtotal	196 0/8
Abnormals	- 10 6/8
Net Non-Typical Score	185 2/8

Big Red and converged on his reported home area in northern Todd County for the gun season that year. C.W. was among the "hundreds." He had decided to spend every minute in pursuit of that buck.

As it turned out, C.W. had an edge over the hordes. A friend from Todd County had seen the buck only two days before and would direct the Bowling Green resident to an area he knew the animal frequented. The chosen stand site was a huge sycamore with big limbs that offered a reasonably comfortable perch. Based on his brief period of scouting and the information provided by his friend, the eager hunter determined that the buck often used a heavy trail that began in a cedar thicket two miles distant and passed just below the sycamore.

With an inside spread of 30 3/8 inches, the Dwight Green Buck, pictured here, shades out the Shelton Buck by an eighth-inch as the widest buck in the B&C records; however, the outside spread of the Shelton Buck is 2 1/2 inches wider. Photo by Dick Idol.

This would be Kentucky's first deer season in 40 years. Because it would last for only one day, there was little doubt in C.W.'s mind that the woods would be full of hunters. He also knew many of them would be after the same buck he was pursuing. Consequently, C.W. and his brother, Rudy, who was from Mayfield, were on their stands by 5 a.m.

It was a damp, overcast morning, and daylight came a little later than usual. In the first hour of the season, C.W. heard many gun shots in the distance, and with each, he wondered if Big Red was already history. On top of that, not long after daylight rain had begun to fall in a steady, rhythmic pattern woodsmen recognize as an all-day event.

After 1 1/2 hours of sitting, C.W. decided to check out the cedar thicket where he felt the buck could be hiding. He still-hunted the two miles to the thicket, then spent another three hours slipping slowly and quietly through the dense evergreens. The buck sign was there, but he saw no deer.

Earlier in the morning, C.W. had heard some shots from the direction of his brother's stand, so now, he decided to check on him. Sure enough, Rudy had shot a buck but had been unable to find it. Together, the brothers spent considerable time tracking the wounded buck, but finally, they lost the faint blood trail in the rain. Though C.W. was somewhat dejected and had given up hope of seeing Big Red, he decided to spend the rest of the day in his sycamore anyway.

At about 2:30 in the afternoon, C.W. heard several shots from the direction of the cedar thicket he'd hunted that morning. A few minutes later, a huge buck came trotting along the trail from the direction of the cedar thicket. As the monster came to a small creek, he stopped for a quick drink. It was then that C.W. got his first good look at the wide, massive rack. As the buck moved along the trail, he disappeared…then suddenly reappeared only 50 yards from the sycamore!

By now, C.W. was experiencing a fair case of buck fever. He fired four shots from his scoped .44 Mag. rifle as the buck bolted. The hunter thought he heard the buck fall in a loud crash about 150 yards away but wasn't sure. C.W.'s mild case of buck fever now turned to pure panic since he wasn't sure how well the buck was hit. Would one of the many other hunters in the area finish off the buck and lay claim to him?

C.W. didn't know what to do, but he didn't want to just sit there. He jumped to the ground, disregarding the limbs normally used for steps, then ran in the direction where he thought the buck was. He found a bloody spot all right, but the buck hadn't stayed down. All was quiet.

Then, C.W. heard another crash. This time, the buck was getting up and running. With his wide rack, he made a tremendous amount of noise as his sweeping beams banged against the trees. C.W. fired several more shots, but the deer kept going.

Though C.W. didn't know it at the time, the buck ran another 200 yards, jumped a big ditch then fell again. After some looking, C.W. couldn't find the

"As the monster came to a small creek, he stopped for a quick drink. It was then that C.W. got his first good look at the wide, massive rack. By now, C.W. was experiencing a fair case of buck fever."

deer. He searched in panic for several minutes, yelling for Rudy all the while. At this point, C.W. thought the buck was gone for good and he actually became physically sick.

Then, with another loud crash, the buck erupted from nearby cover, moving more slowly than before. C.W. ran to within close range and fired two shots that put him down again. By now, the hunter had fired 14 shots and had only one cartridge left. He decided to save this last shell and finish the buck with his knife. Finally, the legend was his.

When Rudy arrived on the scene, he was frantic. After all the yelling and shooting, he didn't know what to expect. But when he saw the giant buck, which eventually dressed 260 pounds, he knew what had happened. For several minutes, both men just stared at the spectacular animal.

Not surprisingly, news about Big Red traveled like wildfire. Back in those days, especially in a community in which deer hunting wasn't an annual occurrence, many sportsmen were uninformed as to the criteria for scoring whitetails. It quickly was reported that in all probability this buck would be a "new world record." What they really meant was that this buck had the widest spread of any whitetail known at the time, and many presumed that would make him the world record. C.W.'s deer was registered officially at 30 2/8 inches inside, which even today is the second-widest inside spread in the B&C record book. Only Dwight Green's 30 3/8-inch Iowa typical, shot the same year, beats Big Red.

Inside spreads don't tell the full story on how wide some deer appear, though, and that's true with this Kentucky trophy. If we go by outside measurement, C.W.'s buck actually is wider than the Iowa giant. Big Red's incredible outside span of 34 4/8 inches—most of that

> *"Big Red's incredible outside span of 34 4/8 inches — most of that on the main beams, not outwardly jutting points — is perhaps the most impressive feature of this rack."*

on the main beams, not outwardly jutting points—is perhaps the most impressive feature of this rack. But not only does he have the spread, tall tines, long beams, great mass and lots of "character" make him one of history's most impressive typical white-tail bucks.

No wonder C.W. got buck fever!

Chapter Thirty-Four

THE CLIFF SMITH BUCK

226 5/8 NON-TYPICAL, MANITOBA, 1980

A Last-Minute Payoff In A "Big" Way

BY GREG MILLER

I'm sure all of us who have the least bit of interest in any sporting event have seen, heard or read about some kind of last-second heroics. Maybe it's a winning shot at the buzzer in a basketball game. Perhaps it's a go-ahead touchdown scored as time is running out in a championship football game. Or maybe, the last-second heroics is a game-winning home run hit with two outs in the bottom of the ninth inning.

Those of us involved in the sport of trophy whitetail hunting know there is such a thing as last-second heroics in our sport also. Many of us have heard stories about how some hunter filled his tag at the last second on the last day of the season. Perhaps some of you reading this have your own 11th-hour success story. Manitoba deer hunter Cliff Smith certainly has his.

Cliff is a farmer who lives near Grand View, Manitoba. As many hunters in Manitoba will tell you, the area around Grand View is not known for its deer hunting. Rather, this area is more renowned for its quality elk hunting. In truth, elk

CLIFF SMITH, MANITOBA, 1980

	Right Antler	Left Antler	Difference
Main Beam Length	26 1/8	26 7/8	6/8
1st Point Length	10 5/8	6 2/8	4 3/8
2nd Point Length	11 4/8	11 4/8	–
3rd Point Length	7 2/8	10 2/8	3 0/8
4th Point Length	12 2/8	10 5/8	1 5/8
5th Point Length	7 2/8	4 5/8	2 5/8
1st Circumference	4 7/8	5 1/8	2/8
2nd Circumference	5 1/8	5 3/8	2/8
3rd Circumference	10 5/8	9 4/8	1 1/8
4th Circumference	6 6/8	6 4/8	2/8
Total	**102 3/8**	**96 5/8**	**14 2/8**

Main Characteristics: Tips of main beams seem to almost touch but one is actually 2" in front of the other. Gross typical score is 214 5/8".

MISCELLANEOUS STATS

No. Of Points–Right	12
No. Of Points–Left	8
Total No. Of Points	20
Length Of Abnormals	26 2/8
Greatest Spread	22 0/8
Tip To Tip Spread	2 0/8
Inside Spread	15 5/8

FINAL TALLY

Inside Spread	15 5/8
Right Antler	102 3/8
Left Antler	96 5/8
Gross Score	214 5/8
Difference	-14 2/8
Subtotal	200 3/8
Abnormals	+26 2/8
NET NON-TYPICAL SCORE	**226 5/8**

hunters are more likely to fill their tags than deer hunters. But, Cliff was not going to let this fact keep him from making an attempt to fill his deer tag.

With the 1980 deer season down to its final day, Cliff decided to give it one last try. Seven others joined him for this do-or-die hunt. Like Cliff, most of these men were area farmers. The hunters had a definite game plan. You see, they had received word that the deer were congregated in the wooded ravines scattered throughout the bush. They also had heard that their best option for getting those deer to move was organized deer drives. This bit of information had been passed along by local hunters Mervin Mitchell and Buster Brownbridge, who earlier had teamed up to take a big non-typical scoring in the 180s.

Weather conditions on the final day of the season were just about perfect for making a hunt. Six to eight inches of snow lay on the ground, while temperatures and wind were about normal for that time of year. But even with the ideal hunting conditions, the hunters had no luck getting the deer to cooperate with their plans. The first half of the day passed without incident.

Then, sometime during mid-afternoon, a doe was pushed out of a piece of bush. One of the standers saw the antlerless deer make its way across a field and into another nearby patch of cover. At this point, the hunters had abandoned hope of shooting a trophy buck and were ready to just settle for some meat for the winter. They decided to go after the doe.

Plans were quickly made as to the best way to push the piece of cover the doe had run into. Drivers and standers were chosen, with Cliff selected to be one of the standers. He was the first to be dropped off and immediately took up his vigil. As he was waiting for the rest of his party to get into position, he noticed some movement in the woods in front of him. Looking closer, Cliff saw a big buck coming right at him!

Apparently, the buck had no idea a hunter was anywhere in the area. The big deer continued to close the distance. He crossed over a fence, entered a nearby field and then turned broadside. At this point, the distance was slightly less than 100 yards. Cliff knew it was now or never. Raising his .22-250 Rem. rifle, he followed the walking buck along for a ways then squeezed off a shot. The hit was quickly fatal, as the big deer traveled a mere 10 yards before tipping over.

Cliff knew something about trophy deer antlers, and as he approached the downed buck, he realized he had just harvested a very exceptional animal. There was not doubt in his mind that he was going to have the rack measured. After the required drying period, Randy Bean, an official measurer from Winnipeg, scored the antlers from Cliff's buck. Randy came up with a score of 223 3/8 non-typical. The buck was declared the largest non-typical recorded in Manitoba for 1980. Sometime later, the rack was rescored by Dave Boland, also a certified measurer. Dave came up with a slightly higher score of 226 5/8 non-typical, and that now stands as the buck's official score.

Cliff's 20-point rack is big in just about every way. The circumference measurements alone add up to a staggering 53 7/8 inches. In addition, six tines measure better than 10 inches. While the inside spread is nothing spectacular at 15 5/8 inches, the main beams measure 26 1/8 and 26 7/8 inches. The basic typical frame of the rack has a world-class gross score of 214 5/8. After side-to-side differences are taken into consideration, the antlers wind up with an impressive net typical score of 200 3/8. Adding in the totals from the eight abnormal points brings the score to 226 5/8 non-typical.

Certainly, harvesting a buck on the last day of the season has to be a great feeling. But, I'm sure that feeling is a bit more special when the deer just happens to be a huge non-typical. Right, Cliff?

"The circumference measurements alone add up to a staggering 53 7/8 inches. In addition, six tines measure better than 10 inches."

Chapter Thirty-Five

THE GARY SMITH BUCK

227 NON-TYPICAL, KANSAS, 1970

The Midwest's Most Massive Monster

BY DICK IDOL

I n recent years, Kansas has received a lot of attention about its big whitetail bucks, and for good reason. Some of the trophies taken there rank among the world's greatest. That certainly can be said of the mammoth non-typical Gary Smith shot back in 1970.

Gary was born and raised in the Paola area of eastern Kansas, and he began deer hunting with his father in 1965, when Gary was 24. From 1965 through '69, Gary opted to bowhunt. While he managed to take a forkhorn and a couple of does, he never arrowed a large buck, though he had opportunity.

In 1970, the frustrated hunter decided to try gun hunting. Gary had worked for Southwestern Bell Telephone Co. since 1958, and his schedule gave him afternoons and weekends to hunt. For two consecutive years, he'd heard rumors of a giant buck haunting an area near a farm belonging to a relative. So before the season, he and his dad went into the area and built a platform stand in a wide hedgerow separating a field from some sparse timber behind it. The stand was back in from the edge to make it less visible and was about 20 feet off the ground.

December 5, the gun opener, was a typically cold, windy day, and Gary and his dad climbed into the platform stand before daylight. The field they would be watching was being used regularly by several deer, as evidenced by the heavy trails and the

GARY SMITH, KANSAS, 1970

	Right Antler	Left Antler	Difference
Main Beam Length	25 7/8	26 6/8	7/8
1st Point Length	8 1/8	8 0/8	1/8
2nd Point Length	9 4/8	4 2/8	5 2/8
3rd Point Length	9 2/8	4 7/8	4 3/8
4th Point Length	–	–	–
5th Point Length	–	–	–
1st Circumference	7 2/8	7 4/8	2/8
2nd Circumference	5 6/8	5 6/8	–
3rd Circumference	10 6/8	10 4/8	2/8
4th Circumference	3 7/8	6 3/8	2 4/8
Total	**80 3/8**	**74 0/8**	**13 5/8**

Main Characteristics: Massive, palmated antlers. Total measurement of all eight circumferences is 57 6/8", for an average circumference of 7 2/8".

MISCELLANEOUS STATS	
No. Of Points–Right	12
No. Of Points–Left	10
Total No. Of Points	22
Length Of Abnormals	62 1/8
Greatest Spread	28 5/8
Tip To Tip Spread	21 2/8
Inside Spread	24 1/8

FINAL TALLY	
Inside Spread	24 1/8
Right Antler	80 3/8
Left Antler	74 0/8
Gross Score	**178 4/8**
Difference	-13 5/8
Subtotal	164 7/8
Abnormals	+62 1/8
NET NON-TYPICAL SCORE	**227 0/8**

plentiful buck sign along the perimeter.

Early morning proved uneventful, however, and at 8 a.m., Gary suggested that perhaps it was time to leave, as they were both very cold. Fortunately, Gary's dad insisted that they remain a little longer.

At 8:30, the elder hunter blurted out, "Look at that big buck over there!" Even though Gary's dad had relatively poor eyesight, he knew he was looking at a big buck nearly 300 yards away in the middle of the field. The buck was walking, stopping frequently to look. He was obvi-

ously nervous and sensed something was wrong.

At the instant the buck was spotted, Gary raised his custom .270 Winchester and scoped the buck through the 3-9X Leupold. And then, he completely lost his cool. The young hunter had never seen anything like this. It was a clear morning, and the buck was walking across the field, offering a good broadside view. The sun was just above the trees and struck the frosted antlers at an angle that illuminated the massive beams.

"My first thought," the hunter later

recalled, "was that he looked like his whole head was ablaze. It was a very strange sight."

Gary knew other hunters were after this buck and that a couple of them were somewhere in the area. What he didn't know, however, was that at that very moment another hunter also was watching the buck. As this unseen hunter moved to get a shot, the buck broke into a trot. Gary was extremely nervous, as was his dad, who kept yelling, "Shoot! Shoot!" Gary finally decided that a 300-yard running shot was all he was going to get.

As the rifle recoiled, Gary saw dirt fly several feet in front of the buck. He knew he had led him too far. But before he could shoot again, the buck, which had become confused by the shot, turned and started running straight toward them. He covered 225 yards in a matter of seconds. All the while the buck raced toward them, Gary's dad was yelling at the top of his lungs, "Shoot! Shoot! Shoot! Shoot!"

The buck was heading for the hedgerow, and if he made it, he would be gone. Gary would have one shot at 75 yards. This time, fortunately, he made good on the opportunity, hitting the buck squarely in the neck. The deer went into a high-speed skid and never regained his feet. Instantly, Gary bailed out of the

Gary Smith holds his massive Kansas buck as his daddy, who "coached" him during the hunt, looks on.
Photo courtesy Gary Smith.

stand and ran toward the buck. By now, Gary's dad had a worse case of buck fever than his son. As the buck kicked for the last time, Gary's dad fired a final shot from the stand.

When Gary got to the downed buck, he realized why the rack looked so strange. It had massive, palmated beams on both sides, with many of the points flattened as well. The rack appeared to be more like that of a moose, instead of a whitetail. Gary was so overwhelmed by the appearance of the buck and the excitement of the hunt that he was still totally speechless when his dad appeared on the scene.

The deer was lean but still dressed 210 pounds. Even so, the antlers were far more impressive. His net score of 227 points placed him third among non-typicals in the state at that time. Clearly, the most impressive feature of Gary's buck is the rack's overall mass. His bases are 7 2/8 and 7 4/8 inches, and his greatest circumferences exceed 10 inches! What's even more astonishing is the fact that the circumferences around the bases of some of his typical points exceed 8 inches! And after all of these years, the rack still weighs more than 10 pounds.

No wonder Gary and his dad suffered such a severe case of buck fever that December morning!

Chapter Thirty-Six

THE HAROLD SMITH BUCK

272 4/8 NON-TYPICAL, BRITISH COLUMBIA, 1951

Whitetail, Mulie or Hybrid?
Huge No Matter The Label

BY DICK IDOL

In 1982, I got word of a giant whitetail killed in British Columbia that had a score in the low 270s. At the time, that would have ranked him in the neighborhood of No. 4 on the all-time non-typical list. I immediately got in my pickup and drove from my home in Montana to Kimberly, British Columbia.

As it turned out, the buck was killed by Harold Smith in 1951 near Toby Creek, which is in the Invermere area. Harold had died in 1956, leaving the head to his wife and son, Randy. His wife didn't hunt and Randy was only nine at the time, so the actual account of the hunt is rather vague.

According to Randy and his mother, they recall Harold describing the fact that the buck was "charging" toward him as he made the shot. Whether or not the buck was actually charging (as some writers have claimed) or simply trailing or coming toward Harold will probably never be known. The fact remains that Harold Smith shot a huge buck in British Columbia in 1951.

For many years, the rack hung in the Smith household without a lot of thought given to score, mounting or notoriety. Then, about 1980, Randy decided to have the head mounted, which lead to its first exposure to the deer fraternity. Obviously, there

HAROLD SMITH, BRITISH COLUMBIA, 1951

	Right Antler	Left Antler	Difference
Main Beam Length	25 7/8	24 6/8	1 1/8
1st Point Length	6 2/8	6 1/8	1/8
2nd Point Length	14 1/8	14 1/8	–
3rd Point Length	13 7/8	12 7/8	1 0/8
4th Point Length	7 0/8	6 2/8	6/8
5th Point Length	–	–	–
1st Circumference	5 1/8	5 2/8	1/8
2nd Circumference	5 3/8	5 3/8	–
3rd Circumference	6 5/8	7 3/8	6/8
4th Circumference	6 3/8	6 6/8	3/8
Total	**90 5/8**	**88 7/8**	**4 2/8**

Main Characteristics: Outside spread of 33 1/8". Inside spread exceeds longest beam and therefore spread credit is only 25 7/8. May be whitetail/ mule deer cross.

MISCELLANEOUS STATS	
No. Of Points–Right	15
No. Of Points–Left	17
Total No. Of Points	32
Length Of Abnormals	71 3/8
Greatest Spread	33 1/8
Tip To Tip Spread	25 0/8
Inside Spread	26 6/8

FINAL TALLY	
Inside Spread	25 7/8
Right Antler	90 5/8
Left Antler	88 7/8
Gross Score	205 3/8
Difference	-4 2/8
Subtotal	201 1/8
Abnormals	+71 3/8
NET NON-TYPICAL SCORE	**272 4/8**

was no cape from the original buck nor any field photos. Randy had always assumed the buck was a whitetail. Consequently, he had the rack mounted with a whitetail cape.

From the onset, there was a question in my mind as to whether this buck was a whitetail, a mule deer or a hybrid. As soon as I held the buck in my hands, I knew one thing for sure—he was huge no matter what the label!

Randy was very straight-forward and made no pretense as to what he was. There was no cape, no photos nor any living eyewitnesses. Any call would simply have to be made from the antlers alone.

After many years of looking at thousands of racks, I've developed a pretty good "feel" for distinguishing between whitetail and mulie racks, but I'll be the first to admit that it's not always a clear-cut case. Contrary to what many think who don't live in mule deer country, a substantial percentage of mulie racks do not have forked back tines, making the distinction more difficult than many might presume.

To determine which species a rack belongs to, I look at four characteristics. In order of their importance, they are: 1) The presence of "cross-beading" and/or the direction of the beading at the bases; 2) The length of the brow tines; 3) Up-sweeping beams; 4) Forked back tines.

When I looked at Harold Smith's buck, my inclination from the beading was definitely mule deer but all the other features leaned toward a whitetail. At six inches, his brow tines would be abnormally long for a mulie. Also arguing for a whitetail origin, his beams do not significantly sweep upwards and he doesn't have classic forked back tines. My ultimate conclusion was that he probably was a hybrid or a mulie, but I would point out that he's one of the toughest calls I've ever seen.

Boone and Crockett has a policy that if a rack is questionable as to its origin or species and documentation, photos, witnesses, hide, etc., are not available, it is

The side views reveal more clearly why there is some question about whether this buck is a mulie, whitetail or a hybrid of the two. The rack, by the way, is not mounted on the deer's original cape.
Photos by Dick Idol.

entered into the classification with the higher minimum qualifying score. In this case, the head has never been submitted to Boone and Crockett, but if they determined that the species is in question, it would be classified as a mulie since that species has a higher minimum.

From the time this buck first came to the surface in the early 1980s, the issue of whether he is a whitetail, a mule deer or a hybrid has been debated. I would contend that, at 272 4/8 non-typical, the main point is he's a giant deer regardless of the species. The minimum for non-typical mule deer is 240. Even if this buck is a mulie, he would rank near No. 60 in the current book and would be the No. 1 non-typical mulie from British Columbia. If he's a whitetail, that would place him in the top 10 all-time non-typicals and make him the best ever from British Columbia. Frankly, neither option is all that bad.

Chapter Thirty-Seven

THE CURT VAN LITH BUCK

197 6/8 TYPICAL, MINNESOTA, 1986

Four-Year Quest For
"The King Of The Corn Field"

BY JEFF MURRAY

It all began on Halloween 1983. Curt Van Lith of Maple Lake, Minnesota, had just arrowed a fat doe after she'd waltzed past his tree stand at the easy range of 12 yards. Just as the hunter was about to climb down from his perch, which overlooked a well-worn trail leading to a scrape, he saw a buck coming down the same path.

The buck was so big, both of body and antler, that Curt did a double take. As he watched in awe, his tag now filled, the monster continued on, heading right for the scrape ... and beyond. As the buck faded from sight, Curt vowed to himself that he'd get another crack at him. No doe or lesser buck would he settle for. After all, he'd taken more than a half-dozen deer with a bow, including a pair of nice bucks. Now, there was a new goal to pursue.

For the remainder of the 1983 deer season, all Curt could do about the buck of his dreams was pray that the slug hunters wouldn't get him. As it turned out, nobody did. Curt began to prepare for 1984.

Prior to the 1984 opener, the bowhunter located the buck's unmistakable tracks—by far the largest in the immediate area—but that year he never got a shot or even a close look at the deer. The season concluded with the buck still leading a charmed life.

The following year, Curt did everything right, according to the books. He scouted

*Main Characteristics:
Massive bow kill from
Minnesota. Gross
score of 217 7/8.*

CURT VAN LITH, MINNESOTA, 1986

	Right Antler	Left Antler	Difference
Main Beam Length	29 1/8	30 2/8	1 1/8
1st Point Length	8 4/8	7 6/8	6/8
2nd Point Length	11 6/8	13 3/8	1 5/8
3rd Point Length	13 5/8	9 2/8	4 3/8
4th Point Length	8 0/8	10 0/8	2 0/8
5th Point Length	–	–	–
1st Circumference	5 7/8	5 7/8	–
2nd Circumference	5 3/8	5 3/8	–
3rd Circumference	13 6/8	7 1/8	6 5/8
4th Circumference	5 1/8	7 2/8	2 1/8
Total	**101 1/8**	**96 2/8**	**18 5/8**

MISCELLANEOUS STATS	
No. Of Points–Right	6
No. Of Points–Left	5
Total No. Of Points	11
Length Of Abnormals	1 4/8
Greatest Spread	23 1/8
Tip To Tip Spread	14 4/8
Inside Spread	20 4/8

FINAL TALLY	
Inside Spread	20 4/8
Right Antler	101 1/8
Left Antler	96 2/8
Gross Score	**217 7/8**
Difference	-18 5/8
Subtotal	199 2/8
Abnormals	-1 4/8
NET TYPICAL SCORE	**197 6/8**

the main rutting territory thoroughly, and he scrutinized the entire home range of the monster whitetail. It was typical Midwest farmland deer country. The section in which the buck left behind the most sign also contained rural homes scattered along a dusty township road. Interspersed among these residences were small woodlots separated by corn and soybean fields.

"Every year, I'd see the same pattern," Curt noted. "The buck would use a main trail bordering one of the woodlots that was touching a corn field my father-in-law had planted. And, 50 to 60 trees, some up to 8 inches in diameter, would be worked over real good in that woodlot, always in the same general area."

During the 1985 season, Curt hunted the most logical place—along that trail bordering the woodlot, where most of the sign was and where he'd first sighted the monster. Yet, the 1985 hunting season closed with the deer remaining completely untouched and mostly unseen, except for two clues to his core territory that had previously eluded Curt.

First, one day during the summer of

1985, the buck was spotted crossing the road, heading into a corn field Curt's father-in-law worked. Later that fall, during the slug season, Curt's brother missed a standing, broadside shot at the deer after he'd been pushed from the same corn patch.

"I just never seriously considered that corn patch," Curt later admitted. "It was only about 20 acres, and there was a house with barking dogs right next to it."

For the 1986 bow season, the hunter had a new plan: He'd start with a clean slate, not letting information gathered from previous years interfere with his objectivity. He wasn't going to overlook anything, no matter how trivial it might seem, that could lead him to the buck's core area. As it turned out, his search wasn't a long one. In August, the first place Curt looked was that corn field, and what he found blew his mind!

As he walked around the edge of the little patch, he saw only small deer prints. But when he moved into the interior, he immediately knew his search was over. The ground was tramped with huge tracks. He had found not only the buck's bedroom, but probably his living and dining rooms as well!

"When I saw all the ruckus he had left behind," Curt recalled, "I got the heck out of there. The last thing I wanted to do was force the buck into another hideout."

Now, the chore was to pinpoint a spot where the buck was likely to enter or exit the corn field during daylight hours. After surveying the layout of the immediate area, Curt zeroed in on a forked elm within a grown-up fence line that bordered the eastern edge of the field. A deer trail passed a scant 10 yards

from the elm. With the September bow opener a full month away, Curt confidently secured his homemade portable stand 18 feet up the tree.

Curt's construction job prevented him from hunting the September 13 bow opener. The next day, a vigil in the elm turned up no deer; neither did continued hunting from that stand during the rainy week that followed. After trying a different stand and fighting more rain during the second week, clear weather finally was forecasted for the third Saturday of the season. Curt would give the old elm one more try.

On the afternoon of September 27, the archer went into his back yard and shot a few arrows with his 60-pound Jennings T Star compound, then showered and headed for the fence line. Parking in an alfalfa field a quarter-mile from the elm stand, Curt sprayed himself with Scent Shield in case he worked up a sweat going into his stand.

After Curt shinnied up the elm, he gave himself one more spray of the odor neutralizer and settled in, expectant of action. But by 6:15 p.m., he was starting to get fidgety. Finally, just as a mourning dove flew overhead, breaking the monotony, the hunter's ears picked up a second noise, a soft rustling in the corn field. Soon, he caught a bit of movement, as antler tips began to move among the corn tassels. Curt's heart raced, his legs shook and his hands trembled. It was him, the king of the corn field!

"I started talking to myself," Curt recalled. "I had to calm myself down, or I wouldn't have a chance for a decent shot."

Slowly, the buck made his way through the corn and toward the fence line. All the while, Curt counted the tines and admired their mass, but he knew he had to avoid getting too excited. When the buck hit the edge of the corn field, he came to a halt and stuck his neck out, testing the wind both ways. It would have been a 30-yard shot, broadside, but Curt had made up his mind he was going to wait for "the sure thing" because the wind was perfect and the buck's trail should lead him to within 15 yards of the stand.

But—and this is a mighty big "but"—the buck stopped coming. He froze, and with a cold, suspecting glare, he looked right up at Curt in the old elm. Finally, he started ambling away, occasionally looking over his shoulder as he did.

Curt couldn't understand how the buck had seen him. He was 18 feet off the ground and hadn't moved a stitch. Subsequently, however, he analyzed the situation and realized that he was partially silhouetted against the sky. The brute must have looked up at that tree often over the years, and when he decided to pass by that day, something seemed out of place. Still, the buck showed no great alarm, just caution.

Fortunately, Curt didn't try to pull off a shot as the deer quartered away, because a "miracle" was about to take place. After crossing the fence line, instead of continuing on in the opposite direction, the big buck turned once again and headed back toward Curt, from the other side of the tree line. He would offer a shot, but this one was going to be nearly 40 yards. The hunter, now fearful that this might be his only chance, got ready to shoot.

As the buck's shoulders appeared through an opening in the tree line, Curt released his arrow. Immediately after the shot, the huge deer hunched up and romped into the woods, making a racket down in the brush.

"I headed for my pickup," Curt said. "I would need a flashlight in case the deer went farther than expected. Plus, I needed to get out of all those clothes, because I knew I wasn't going to get cold looking for that monster."

As the hunter left his pickup, his wife's uncle saw him heading back down the alfalfa field. Curt told him he'd just shot the huge buck. Unfortunately, shortly after Curt arrived back at his stand, a bunch of family members and neighbors showed up on 3-wheelers. They only meant to help with the recovery of the deer, but when the wounded buck heard the commotion, he pushed the panic button.

At first, the heavy blood trail was easy to follow. The buck doubled back across the township road, bounding it in a single leap. There was so much blood where he landed on the opposite side that everyone seemed convinced that the search soon would be over. A good blood trail continued, enabling the crew to shadow the buck as he led them to a bean field and into a corn field.

Then, the tracks did something strange—they ran up and down every row. The gang spent over an hour in that field alone, sorting out the sign. The trail then headed for another bean field, and now, the distance between tracks widened, indicating that the buck was picking up steam. Eventually, the blood trail dwindled to nothing, making further tracking in the dark next to impossible. It now was midnight, and the search was reluctantly halted.

The next morning, the chase resumed. Aided by two assistants, Curt found that the only way to continue the pursuit was by having his helpers stand at the last identified mark while he searched ahead for the next one. The faint trail led to a small thicket, where the trio found a globule of fat stuck to some tall grass. At this point, blood began to flow again. The trail revealed that the buck had gone through a fence sectioning off a horse pasture then into yet another woodlot.

"There was a pond in the woodlot that had a half-submerged barbed-wire fence running down the middle of it," Curt noted. "This almost threw us off, because we could not imagine an injured deer trying to go through it. But, after searching the rest of the woodlot without turning up any evidence, we returned to the pond. Sure enough, we could barely make out that the buck had muscled his way right through the middle, instead of going around it."

A heavy blood trail continued into a corn field, where the buck had bedded. The spot was torn up, suggesting that he'd had a tough time getting to his feet again. Then, the trail led to a second corn

Shown here with his buck, Curt Van Lith hunted hard over a four-year period before finally connecting with the great typical. Photo courtesy Curt Van Lith.

field, where Curt finally spotted his dream buck bedded. Another arrow to the neck (the only visible target) and then another behind the shoulders finally felled the huge deer.

The hunt was over, but the suspense wasn't. Soon after the kill, veteran measurer Dave Boland looked at the buck and immediately recognized him as a potential archery state-record typical. However, Dave knew a judgment call would have to be made on what appeared to be "fused" G-2 and G-3 tines on the right antler. If the judges' panel considered those tines as separate typical points, the final score would be just under 200 net points. If considered as one typical tine with a fork off it, the rack would score closer to 160, because it would essentially be ruled a basic 4x4 typical with heavy deductions.

Fortunately, the Pope and Young judges' panel gave the rack a favorable ruling, and the final score ended up at 197 6/8. That tied the Van Lith Buck with Lloyd Goad's 1962 buck from Iowa at No. 2 on bowhunting's all-time list of typical whitetails, justly rewarding Curt's four-year quest. Of such stuff are legendary whitetails truly made!

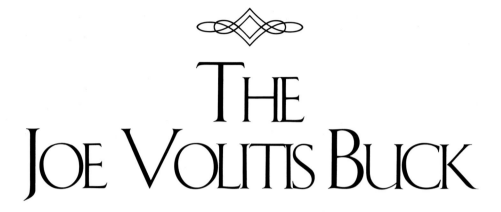

Chapter Thirty-Eight

THE JOE VOLITIS BUCK

180 5/8 TYPICAL, WEST VIRGINIA, 1969

The Shocker From The Appalachian Mountaintops

BY DICK IDOL

Although few outsiders know it, remnants of a "Daniel Boone" culture still hang on today deep in the heart of the rugged mountains of West Virginia. There, vine-covered barns and ancient log cabins sit serenely along narrow, winding roads, serving as reminders of a fading era. In this part of the world, a big buck is more likely to find his way into the larder than into the record book.

Residents such as Joe Volitis have long been serious hunters, though, and they spend as much time as possible in the woods, hunting whatever's in season.

"My buddies and I have hunted these mountains most of our lives," Joe told me. "We start turkey hunting in October, and that's when we do most of our scouting for whitetails. Luckily, some of the best turkey and deer hunting occurs in the same area, so we are constantly scouting for both when hunting either one.

"We do all our hunting near the very tops of the mountains," Joe noted. "Nowadays, we have to go to the most rugged and inaccessible areas to find the bigger, older bucks. Years ago, lots of big bucks could be found around farms and orchards near the valley floor, but because the hunting pressure has increased so much, the really big ones are most often found in the most difficult places to hunt, like mountaintops. I especially like to be near rock cliffs with heavy, jungle-like mountain laurel around. Even when cliffs are not present where we hunt, the terrain

Photo by Ron Brown

Main Characteristics: Great Eastern U.S. typical. Drop tine on right side helps looks, hurts score.

JOE VOLITIS, WEST VIRGINIA, 1969

	Right Antler	Left Antler	Difference
Main Beam Length	25 0/8	23 6/8	1 2/8
1st Point Length	7 1/8	5 5/8	1 4/8
2nd Point Length	13 6/8	14 0/8	2/8
3rd Point Length	11 3/8	11 3/8	–
4th Point Length	8 2/8	8 5/8	3/8
5th Point Length	–	–	–
1st Circumference	5 3/8	5 3/8	–
2nd Circumference	4 7/8	4 7/8	–
3rd Circumference	5 3/8	5 5/8	2/8
4th Circumference	5 4/8	5 4/8	–
Total	**86 5/8**	**84 6/8**	**3 5/8**

MISCELLANEOUS STATS	
No. Of Points–Right	7
No. Of Points–Left	6
Total No. Of Points	13
Length Of Abnormals	10 4/8
Greatest Spread	24 6/8
Tip To Tip Spread	23 3/8
Inside Spread	23 3/8

FINAL TALLY	
Inside Spread	23 3/8
Right Antler	86 5/8
Left Antler	84 6/8
Gross Score	194 6/8
Difference	-3 5/8
Subtotal	191 1/8
Abnormals	-10 4/8
NET TYPICAL SCORE	180 5/8

is usually very steep, rocky and thick, except where the laurel thickets are absent under the canopy of tall oaks and other hardwoods. Most of these reclusive mountain bucks spend their entire life in this rough, high country and seldom travel to the valley floor for the more lush feed."

Early in the fall of 1969, while Joe and his buddies hunted turkeys high up on Cheat Mountain, they found some huge rubs and tracks they assumed had been made by a big buck. Although no one in the party actually saw the animal,

they decided this was the place to spend opening day of deer season.

Before dawn on opening day of the 1969 deer season, Joe and three buddies gathered to eat breakfast. They had already decided where each hunter would sit, so after their meal, they undertook the long and jarring ride up an old tram road to the top. From there, each man walked quietly to his predetermined stand site.

"It's important," Joe told me later, "to scout out an area very thoroughly. You need to know the terrain inside and out and learn all the bedding areas and where all the deer trails go. During most of West Virginia's season, acorns or mast will be the primary diet of mountain bucks. Find the best acorn ridges and you'll find where the deer are feeding. Trails usually will leave these feeding areas and lead back into large laurel jungles. I like to find where a trail enters a thicket that has a concentration of rubs and scrapes scattered around. Bucks move fairly rapidly along trails through the open timber, but just in the edge of the thickets, they mill around and leave sign. I never use a tree stand. The terrain is so steep I can usually find a good vantage point on a rock outcrop or steep ridge."

On this particular cold, December morning, he settled back against a rough-barked white oak trunk to await dawn. Quietly feeding handloads into his trusted .280 Remington bolt-action, the veteran hunter had a good feeling about the spot.

Joe's morning was fairly uneventful, but from the several nearby shots he'd heard, he suspected one of his partners might have done better. Each man carried his own portable two-way radio, which was used for communicating when help was needed to drag out a deer or to find a lost hunter. (In West Virginia, such radios are legal to use while hunting.) With the radio, Joe learned at lunchtime that one of his friends had indeed connected on a nice buck.

At about 3 p.m., Joe was scanning the woods for deer when he heard a shot just above him, followed by a loud yell from a buddy, "Joe, a huge buck is coming your way!"

The loud crashes of the buck were indeed coming directly toward Joe, but he could see only the whipping laurel tops as the deer approached him. Finally, the buck burst into open woods, and Joe saw the enormous rack for the first time. He hurriedly squeezed off a shot as the running deer disappeared. Seconds later, Joe could hear the monster buck crashing on down the mountainside, but he wasn't sure if he'd made a good hit or not. Immediately, the excited hunter took off down the mountain after the buck. Gasping for breath, Joe soon spotted the buck peering at him from a thicket. A clean neck shot finished him off and brought the chase to an end.

Just then, Joe's buddy who'd yelled came rushing up and excitedly asked, "Did you get him?"

"I think so," Joe replied, as he pointed into the thicket.

Joe's first sight of the huge rack reminded him of an elk. He'd killed a big 11-pointer and several other good bucks, but this was the biggest rack he'd ever laid eyes on—dead or alive!

The next day, the buck was hung at a local service station in Joe's nearby hometown of Elkins. The station owner reported having his best day of business ever. As Joe pointed out, "It was certainly the biggest buck 'most anyone had seen around these parts. The official dressed weight was 287 pounds, and the biologist estimated his age at only 3 1/2 years old!"

At 180 5/8 typical, the Volitis Buck is unquestionably one of the finest typicals ever killed east of the Mississippi River. But, don't be surprised if someday another hunter pulls an even bigger deer off the top of one of West Virginia's rugged mountains.

Chapter Thirty-Nine

THE SAMMY WALKER BUCK

UNSCORABLE, LOUISIANA, 1958

The Bizarre Buck Of Bayou Blue

BY DICK IDOL

Sammy H. Walker—"Peanut" to his friends—stared in amazement at the approaching animal. He thought it was a deer, but he really wasn't sure! The dogs were close, and this "thing" was running flat out as it crossed the narrow logging road. The body appeared to be that of a deer, but on its head was a pile of something that caused the animal to look more like an apparition than a whitetail buck. Besides the apparent mass of antlers jutting in every direction, broken tree branches also adorned the head. To top it off, the entire mess was laced with vines, which draped in long streams alongside the body.

Well, whatever it was, Peanut decided he was going to shoot it.

Like his father before him, Peanut grew up in the outdoors as a houndsman and deer hunter—in that order. These days it's popular to bash the sport of hunting deer with dogs, but those who haven't experienced this rich and ancient ritual firsthand, should temper their criticism with understanding. For one thing, dogging deer primarily evolved in the Deep South in areas where the habitat is not conducive to conventional tactics. Vast stretches of swampland with heavy timber and lush underbrush that remains green all year comprise a substantial portion of this habitat. Even walking can be difficult, and visibility is nearly nil. For decades, the use of hounds to move whitetails was the most common way of hunting these places.

Of course, hunting traditions, cultures, tactics and habitats themselves are changing, and not in favor of dog hunting for deer. The biggest problem lies in the fact that

hounds can't read "Posted" signs. With so much land now having been broken into smaller tracts, the deer hound is now a far less popular fellow than he once was.

Back in the 1950s, however, hunting with dogs was the thing to do in Louisiana, and Peanut liked nothing better. He'd gather up his sons, friends and hounds each weekend of the deer season, and they'd hunt every hour possible. Peanut's two redbones and two Walker hounds were good and fast.

For much of his life, Peanut had hunted the bayous and swamps in the parish of Grosse Tete, and he knew many of the backwater areas well. One of his favorites for bucks was Bayou Blue, which most local folks simply called "Bay Blue." On January 2, 1958, his hunting party headed there.

For more than one reason, this was not a normal day. The South was in the grip of a bitter cold spell, as the temperature had dropped to 20 degrees. (Trust me when I say that 20 degrees in Louisiana's humidity is "bitter.") To make conditions even worse, an ice storm had hit the area the previous day, coating the brush with a heavy glaze. This was real winter in the Deep South!

But, Peanut was confident, for he knew Bay Blue inside and out. Great knowledge of the land and deer patterns is actually of vital importance in dog hunting, because quite often, bucks (more so than does) will be so far ahead of the dogs that they'll cross roads or other potential ambush sites long before the dogs are even within hearing distance of hunters stationed at those points. It's critical to know which crossings the deer favor, and in this area, Peanut did.

About first light, he drove his pickup down a rough back road to a spot where he knew whitetails had been feeding on winter wheat. Peanut figured that in the sticky, black "gumbo" mud of the field he might find a big, fresh track for the hounds to follow. And that he did. Not long after daybreak, the hunter spotted a big track and dropped the tailgate for the four dogs to begin doing their thing.

The cold-trailing continued for several minutes, as the howls came sporadically in long, drawn-out notes. Then, all at once, the pace picked up and excited, choppy tones blended into one high-pitched chorus. The buck had been jumped, and the race was on.

As the dogs went in one direction, Peanut took his clan in the other. He quickly dropped off standers at favorite crossings and eventually posted on the last one himself. In the distance, he could hear the dogs making their way through the swamp. Excitement was heavy in the air, as frozen limbs cracked with the slightest breeze.

The dogs seemed to turn Peanut's way, so he peered hard in their direction. Then, a quick flash to the hunter's right startled him, but it turned out to be only a pair of wrens chasing each other through the limbs of a small cypress tree. The wait continued.

Soon the dogs were close, and Peanut knew the deer had to be as well. But except for the hounds, there was silence all around. Then suddenly, a mass of antlers and vegetation bounced over the tops of the frozen brush. Quickly overcoming the shock of what he saw, Peanut slipped off the safety of his Stevens 12-gauge pump shotgun and fired one shot as the buck crossed the right-of-way. The deer was broadside, and the buckshot found its mark, causing the beast to drop in his tracks.

As Peanut began his walk up to the buck, he still wasn't sure what he'd shot. The branches and trailing vines entangled in the deer's rack indeed made for a sight few hunters have ever witnessed. After careful examination, he found he'd killed a buck with a bizarre set of antlers. For quite a while, he was the talk of Bay Blue since nobody had ever seen anything like this deer. The buck also was exceptionally large-bodied.

When the deer was killed, his rack was covered in velvet, meaning he was almost certainly a "cactus" buck, or "stag" (a buck without testicles). Although there's a widespread belief that such bucks usually have been castrated while jumping fences or going through thick brush, most "stags" actually are born without testicles. These bucks obviously don't breed or get involved in the rut and are basically social outcasts. The antlers never shed their velvet; nor are the antlers ever dropped.

Characteristically, antlers on such bucks have an overabundance of points and they almost always lack a well-defined typical frame. But even though I've seen many such racks in the past, I've yet to see another with the drooping

As deer enthusiast Roger Selner shows off this bizarre buck, imagine what Sammy Walker must have thought when his dogs pushed this deer into the sights of his shotgun. Photo courtesy Roger Selner.

appearance and sheer amount of bone Peanut's buck displays. Overall, this is certainly one of the most unusual racks ever.

The odd nature of the rack also makes it a scorer's nightmare. It has been scored by veteran Boone and Crockett measurer Dave Boland at 291 3/8 non-typical points. But even as Dave taped the rack, he noted that the buck could be rejected for entry because B&C has a rule against accepting antlers from "cactus" bucks. Even if that wasn't a problem with this deer, it certainly would be hard to identify which parts of the rack (if any) are the main beams. Without main beams, there can't be a measurement of inside spread; nor can a person determine where to place the tape for circumference measurements. Even so, without counting any main beams, inside spread or circumferences, this rack has 190 3/8 inches of measurements, and it weighs more than 10 pounds!

Regardless of what anyone else decides regarding this monster's actual score, he definitely makes Peanut Walker's "book." Shooting him was the highlight of this sportsman's many years of whitetail hunting, and chances are this legendary whitetail will forever be known as the biggest buck to come from Bay Blue.

Chapter Forty

THE JEFFERY WHISKER BUCK

191 TYPICAL, IOWA, 1993

A Wonderful Case Of Mistaken Identity

BY BILL WINKE

Jeffery Whisker's job as a rural mail carrier in eastern Iowa helped put him in position to shoot one of bowhunting's finest typical whitetails ever.

"If I had turned around at the driveway on the top of the hill at the end of that part of my route, I would never have seen the buck," Jeffery later admitted. "It was a dangerous hill, so I'd go past it to turn around. Well, for at least a month straight in January and February of 1993, I saw this wide, heavy buck bedded among some small saplings in exactly the same spot each time I drove down the hill to turn around. He was about 150 yards away, so I never got a real good look at him, but I knew he was easily the biggest buck I had ever seen. I really wanted to get a crack at him in the fall.

"I decided I would try to get the buck with a bow when the season opened in October, so I went out and bought a new Pearson Renegade compound bow, a release, sights—the whole works. I practiced shooting all summer. I would intentionally draw my bow while pointing away from the target and then slowly bring it around until it was aimed right where I wanted to hit, just as if it were a real deer. I wanted my shooting to be instinctive."

Jeffery scouted the whole area looking for the best stand site. The limited cover in the two-square-mile area consisted of a dense, 100-acre woodlot (off-limits to hunt-

Photo by Ron Brown

Jeffery Whisker, Iowa, 1993

	Right Antler	Left Antler	Difference
Main Beam Length	28 1/8	27 1/8	1 0/8
1st Point Length	5 4/8	4 7/8	5/8
2nd Point Length	14 7/8	13 5/8	1 2/8
3rd Point Length	13 3/8	13 4/8	1/8
4th Point Length	7 0/8	8 5/8	1 5/8
5th Point Length	–	–	–
1st Circumference	5 7/8	5 7/8	–
2nd Circumference	4 6/8	5 2/8	4/8
3rd Circumference	4 7/8	5 3/8	4/8
4th Circumference	4 3/8	4 4/8	1/8
Total	**88 6/8**	**88 6/8**	**5 6/8**

Main Characteristics: Classic 5x5 bow kill from Iowa with extremely long G-2s and G-3s, all over 13 inches.

Miscellaneous Stats	
No. Of Points–Right	5
No. Of Points–Left	6
Total No. Of Points	11
Length Of Abnormals	1 0/8
Greatest Spread	22 4/8
Tip To Tip Spread	10 5/8
Inside Spread	20 2/8

Final Tally	
Inside Spread	20 2/8
Right Antler	88 6/8
Left Antler	88 6/8
Gross Score	197 6/8
Difference	-5 6/8
Subtotal	192 0/8
Abnormals	-1 0/8
Net Typical Score	191 0/8

ing), a lot of standing corn fields, a couple of medium-sized woodlots of 5 to 15 acres and one very small woodlot. As Jeffery studied the area, one place in particular caught his eye—a fence line connecting the no-hunting area to one of the medium-sized woodlots. This woodlot was especially thick and was surely serving as a bedding area. Right along this fence line was a tiny, quarter-acre woodlot. It seemed the perfect ambush point for intercepting a big buck moving between the two bedding areas.

"There was a wide trail and two large scrapes right along the fence line, where it formed the upper edge of the little woodlot," Jeffery noted. "There were also a couple of big rubs on trees along the fence, showing that a big buck was using the trail. I figured this would be as good a spot as any to try to take the big buck. I put my stand up 14 feet high, about 12 yards from the trail, and cut two shooting lanes.

"Next, I needed to figure out the best way to get in and out of the stand without leaving too much scent or spooking any deer in the standing corn," Jeffery said. "I got permission to park in the neighboring farmer's yard and slip through the standing corn right up to the fence at the upper edge of the little woodlot. I then crossed the fence and the trail and went the short distance to my stand. I figured any deer that hit my scent would stop in a place that would give me a shot. Coming in from below, I would have had to pass through too much standing corn, possibly spooking deer. I took a chance that my rubber boots and scent-free clothing would keep my trail from being scented too much.

"I knew I needed to get the buck before the corn was picked. I didn't figure he would travel open fields to get to the woodlot during the day. For this reason, I hunted the area hard during October," the bowhunter explained.

The strategy worked. Jeffery was able to hunt the stand several times in early October of 1993, seeing many deer. Then, his chance at the big one came.

"October 17 was warm and sunny," he recalled. "It was probably 55 degrees when I got off work. I changed into my hunting clothes that I kept in a plastic bag and headed for the stand on the fence line. I got into my stand around 4 o'clock. I was facing straight west into the setting sun, with the fence running north and south right in front of me and standing corn on all sides of the tiny woodlot. It was really weird hunting there because deer just materialized out of nowhere from the standing corn.

"Around 6 o'clock, I heard a deer coming. I drew my bow and aimed straight at the rub I figured a buck would stop to work," Jeffery remembered. "It was a decent buck, but he kept right on going. That's when I heard something

else coming from the same direction, from toward the sanctuary. I glanced back to the right, and my heart skipped a beat. There he was, walking right down the trail. The first buck was pretty good, but this one was unbelievable!

"I carefully brought the bow around until the pin was right where I wanted the arrow to go. I squeezed the trigger on the release and heard the arrow hit. It appeared to go right through his lungs for a solid, low-chest hit. The buck took two giant lunges and was up over the little hill to my left and racing through the rest of the woodlot. When he hit the corn field, I could hear the stalks smashing out of his way. Then, there was a crash and everything was silent.

"I'll remember those few electrified seconds all my life. After that, I simply came unglued. I was gasping for air; I was in shock! I knew what my ears had told me, and I looked down to see that the arrow was gone. I thought to myself, God, please let this be true! I just couldn't believe it had actually happened.

"I knew exactly where the buck had gone down, so five minutes later, I dared to try climbing down. I never bothered to follow the blood trail," Jeffery noted. "I just walked right to him, 80 yards away.

"I just stood there with my mouth hanging open and looked for the longest time," Jeffery recalled. "Finally, I walked over and grabbed his horns and started counting. I was awed. Then it dawned on me—this wasn't the buck I had seen during the winter! That buck had been a lot wider and not quite as tall."

But, Jeffery didn't mind getting a buck other than the one he'd gone after. With a score of 191, his buck ranks No. 8 all time among archery typicals!

CONCLUSION

BY DICK IDOL

The popularity of whitetail deer and whitetail hunting is certainly no new revelation. This adaptable animal of wilderness, farmland and suburbs is hands down America's most popular big game, but the mystique surrounding big bucks extends far beyond the mere sport of hunting.

A great deal of this special reverence has to do with the profoundly unique antlers carried by the bucks. Bass fishing and turkey hunting are certainly popular activities, and a 10-pound-plus bass or a gobbler with a 12-inch beard are trophy standards well recognized by fishermen or hunters interested in those respective species. But, neither trophy carries the same personal identity and physical uniqueness as the equivalent 170-point whitetail buck.

Each trophy buck not only sports a set of antlers unlike any other in the world, but they have a permanence not found in fish or birds. Historically, man has collected skulls, teeth, shells, claws, horns, antlers and other game parts as souvenirs and mementos of various experiences, or simply for decor. Antlers and horns have always been among the most popular of these, and for the last two decades, large and unique whitetail racks have evoked a fascination unprecedented in history.

At the heart of the special aurora surrounding big bucks and whitetail hunting are the legends. While each set of antlers is as unique as an original piece of art, their distinctiveness and attraction become far more profound as racks become larger. In most cases, the antlers of the greatest bucks in the world are so unique that they are routinely recognized by a large percentage of the "whitetail fraternity."

Not only have the antlers themselves become legend, but so have the individuals involved and their stories. At this point in time, we can look back over more than a century's worth of history to glean out those special bucks and their remarkable stories. Each of the great bucks featured in this book are a part of hunting history, and many of these bucks enjoy a level of fame unprecedented in the outdoor world.

Dick Idol uncovered and brought to public attention many of the bucks featured in this book, the most famous of which is the Hole-In-The-Horn. Photo courtesy Dick Idol.

significant monuments of our whitetail hunting history and heritage. He genuinely desires to protect these priceless trophies and to make them available to the public so all who appreciate them can enjoy their majesty.

For nearly 15 years, David Morris and I have shared a common interest in these great bucks and their stories through *North American WHITETAIL,* a

Compiling the stories of these great bucks has been a labor of love for me for more than 30 years. Before I was even old enough to hunt, big bucks held a special fascination for me. That fascination has since become my career, love, job, hobby and life's work. It has been a wonderful and enjoyable journey!

Over the years, I've owned many of the great heads featured in these pages, and I'm elated to pass the torch to Larry Huffman, who now is the owner of the Legendary Whitetail Collection. Larry shares my special feelings toward these

magazine that he and I co-founded, along with Steve Vaughn. It seemed only natural that Larry Huffman, David Morris and myself would join forces to put this book together. With the help of several other talented writers, we have compiled a book that provides a window back in time and a look at many of the most legendary whitetails of the last 100 or more years. The photos in this book represent the visual images of our most fanciful dreams, and the stories behind them verify that it could happen to us!